Monographs
of the
American Jewish Archives
Number 9

Jacob R. Marcus
and Abraham J. Peck
Editors

A Century of Memories, 1882-1982

The
East European
Jewish
Experience in
America

Edited by Uri D. Herscher

American Jewish Archives

*On the Cincinnati Campus of the Hebrew Union College –
Jewish Institute of Religion*

Library of Congress Cataloging in Publication Data
Main entry under title:
The East European Jewish experience in America.
(Monographs of the American Jewish Archives; no. 9)
Includes bibliographical references and index.
1. Jews, East European – United States – Biography.
2. Jews – United States – Biography. 3 United States
– Emigration and immigration – Biography. I. Herscher,
Uri D. II. Series.
E184.J5E19   1983   973'.04924022 [B]   83-6416
ISBN 0-87820-011-8

Designed by Noel Martin
Manufactured in the United States of America

Frontispiece: The Statue of Liberty:
America's Symbol of Hope (Photo by Bill Aron)

Table of Contents

A contemporary aerial view of New York's Lower East Side
(Photo by Bill Aron)

*T*his volume owes a great deal to my parents,
Joseph and Lucy Herscher. Refugees from Nazi persecution,
they have personified to me since my early youth that
blend of courage, hope and pride, tested in adversity, which also
marked Jewish immigrants of an earlier day.

*A*cknowledgments: In editing this volume, I had the support of a number of people. Dr. Alfred Gottschalk, president of Hebrew Union College-Jewish Institute of Religion, and Professor Jacob R. Marcus, director of the American Jewish Archives, gave me every encouragement. Dr. Stanley F. Chyet, professor of American Jewish History on the Los Angeles campus of the College-Institute and Dr. Abraham Peck, associate director of the American Jewish Archives, continually offered me their resourceful expertise.

Introduction

Being an immigrant myself, I have an insatiable curiosity about the experience of other immigrants. My own family is of Central European origin. But from Eastern Europe, and particularly from what before 1917 had been the tsarist empire, the majority of Jewish émigrés have come to America during the past hundred years, and so, almost inevitably, my own explorations have been focused on what eighty years ago an often puzzled German-oriented American Jewish community disdainfully called the "Russians" — to the dismay of the Poles and Lithuanians and Ukrainians and Byelorussians and Moldavians among the immigrants from the tsarist realm. Of course, these immigrants commonly assuaged their wounded pride by referring contemptuously to their Central European predecessors here, a mixed multitude of Rhinelanders, Prussians, Bavarians, Alsatians, Austrians, Bohemians, Germanized Magyars, Prussianized Western Poles, Silesians, and Galicians, as *daitchen* — "Germans." The confrontation, or maybe it would be closer to reality to say, the misunderstanding, simply confirms that the biblical saying "its ways are ways of pleasantness and all its paths are peace" applies only at rare intervals to Jewish communal affairs.[1]

Few of the Jewish immigrants to America truly knew what kind of land and society awaited them. One configuration loomed large in their expectations. Nothing sums it up better than the epithet the immigrants used for America before they arrived here. America beckoned to them, to their imagination, as the *goldene medineh*, the Golden Land. Some of them, it is said, fully expected to find American streets paved with gold. I think not many of them, if indeed any, were quite so naive. They rather thought of a society golden in the social and economic opportunities it offered and in the political liberty which its citizens enjoyed.

In Russia, the government was the enemy of the Jews. It treated its Jewish subjects like pariahs, concocting a devil's brew of disabilities to restrict Jewish residential rights and Jewish economic activity. Especially from the 1880's on, as the empire's economic crisis deepened, Jews were subjected to pogroms, explusions, confiscatory taxation — whatever indeed could demonstrate the tsarist regime's view of them as, in the words of one high-ranking official, the "Hebrew leprosy." No wonder some two million Jews fled Russia between the 1880's and the outbreak of World War I. The tsars, blessedly different in this respect from their Soviet successors, encouraged the exodus. An American consul stationed in the tsarist capital reported in the mid-1880's that "the Government is well satisfied and even anxious to get rid of its Israelite population and when (the Jews) go it is not with a blessing but with a kick and 'glad to get rid of you'." One of Tsar Alexander III's closest associates is said to have proposed that Russia's "Jewish problem" be solved by forcing a third of the Jewish population to emigrate, requiring a third to accept baptism, and allowing the remaining third to starve to death.[2]

But it was not only from peasant pogromists and from tsarist officials that such intolerance came. Even a presumably anti-tsarist radical spokesman might contemplate with pleasure the undoing of the Jews. The revolutionary Narodniki (Populists) urged their followers to "wreak . . . vengence on the landowners; *pillage the Jews;* kill the (tsar's) officials!" Is it any wonder that so many Jews left their familiar habitat and turned their backs forever on Eastern Europe.[3]

They were remarkable people, these Jews who took it upon themselves to quit Stepmother Russia and cross the Atlantic to the Golden West. They were an extraordinary breed: a blend of utopian idealism and the courage to brave uncertainty. Within a few weeks or at most a few months, they exchanged a largely agrarian medieval society for the Western world's urban-industrial frontier, the faltering feudal economy of Eastern Europe for the burgeoning industrial capitalism of North America. Initially, to be sure, it seemed as though they had exchanged the misery of their *shtetlach,* their East European villages, for the misery of grimy ghettoes in New York and Boston and Philadelphia. But as the social reformer Jacob Riis observed, "nowhere in the world" were "so many people crowded together in one square mile as here" on the Lower East Side of New York City, and yet, its poverty and filth notwithstanding, the neighborhood was, according to Riis, "the healthiest spot in the city" due to "the temperate habits of the Jew and his freedom from enfeebling vices."[4] The proletarian writer Michael Gold would recall his own experience as a child with immigrants newly arrived on New York's Lower East Side:

> When I woke of a morning, I was never greatly surprised to find in my bed a new family of immigrants in their foreign baggy underwear.... Around the room was scattered their wealth, all their striped calico seabags ... featherbeds, pots, pans, fine peasant linen.... Every tenement was a Plymouth Rock like ours. The hospitality was taken for granted until a new family rented its own flat. The immigrants would sit around our supper table, and ask endless questions about America.... They would walk up and down our East Side Street, peering at policemen and saloons in amazement at America. They would make discoveries: they would chatter and be foolish. After a few days they left us with thanks.[5]

Not a few immigrants never made it in the New World. But what was most characteristic was not lasting bewilderment but a determination to rise in the world, to make the New World of America into a *goldene medineh* for themselves and their children. Sholom Aleichem's Tevye had a son-in-law who believed that "a poor man was far more important than a rich one" and that money was "the source of all falsehood." Such beliefs were certainly not lacking among the immigrants, but the typical immigrant had different ideas. Alfred Kazin wrote of the public school he attended in Brownsville: "It was never learning I associated with that school: only the necessity to succeed, to get ahead ... in the daily struggle to 'make a good impression' on our [Anglo-Saxon] teachers who ... never stopped trying to dig out of us whatever small morsel of fact we had managed to get down the night before. We had to prove that we were really alert, ready for anything, always in the race." It does not sound very attractive or very edifying, that race, but these remarkable runners included, after all, Kazin himself.[6]

In his autobiographical volume, *New York Jew,* Kazin asks: When did the Jews lose "their martial strength and ancient stoniness?" And he answers: when Judaism "became the weeping religion of powerlessness in their exile."[7] That is saying too much even for Jews who remained in Eastern Europe. It is very much at odds with the spirit which could be seen among Jewish immigrants settled in America. Rabbi David Philipson, a native Midwesterner and a member of the Hebrew Union College's first graduating class in the 1880's, recorded in his diary an episode which amused him but which can be read as more than comedy:

> Cincinnati, September 25, 1905
> I had an amusing experience this morning which showed me that "muscular Judaism" is not non-existent. Several weeks ago I preached a sermon [against] Bible teaching in public schools. This sermon called forth a vicious attack by a Presbyterian minister by the name of Macauley, who was reported to have said among other things that he did not blame the Russians for the manner in which they treated the Jews. This almost incredible statement on the part of a Christian minister aroused the keenest indignation on the part of the Jews. One of them, a teacher of athletics, Morris Isaacs by name, met me this morning and told me that he had written Macauley a letter which that gentleman would not readily publish to the world. In that letter he had told him what he thought of him and had advised him to cease from troubling Dr. P[hilipson]. He, Isaacs, would be glad to meet him anywhere and at any time and would encounter him as he might choose, "with or without gloves."[8]

Generally, pride in their Jewishness and willingness to stand up for it were characteristic of the immigrants' newly acquired American stance. Most of them did not lose themselves; they retained their religio-ethnic identity. In time they would create an amalgam of American and East European Jewish values, and *that* is the point: it was, it continues to be, an amalgam, for they did not melt away into America; instead, as the memoirs assembled in this volume testify, they let America melt into them.

However, illustrating that process is not the first or predominant purpose of this collection. Rather, its main aim is to show how different kinds of people — men and women, children and adults, little educated and more sophisticated persons — reacted to and expressed the "immigrant experience," and to supplement their story with the accounts of a few others who dealt professionally with immigrants. In making the selection no systematic methodology was employed. Without changing or editing their language, memoirs and reports were included because in each the "immigrant experience" seemed to be mirrored in a special way. Together, it is hoped, they will convey an impression of the wide variety of that experience — its different settings, tone, and outlook — and serve to instruct as well as entertain.[9]

Uri D. Herscher
Los Angeles, California
April, 1982

Notes

1. See J. R. Marcus, "Background," in O. I. Janowsky, ed., *The American Jew: A Reappraisal* (Philadelphia, 1964), pp. 9-10; Z. Szajkowski, "The Attitude of American Jews to East European Immigration," in *Publications of the American Jewish Historical Society [PAJHS]*, XL (1950-51), 221 ff.: Arthur A. Goren, *New York Jews and the Quest for Community* (New York, 1970), pp. 21 ff.

2. See *PAJHS*, XXXVI (1943), 171 ff.; Louis Greenberg, *The Jews in Russia: The Struggle for Emancipation* (New Haven, 1951), II, 19 ff., 55 ff.; Evan R. Chesler, *The Russian Jewry Reader* (New York, 1974), pp. 25 ff.; S. M. Dubnow, *History of the Jews in Russia and Poland* (Philadelphia, 1918), II, 243 ff.; W. P. Dillingham *et al.* (The Immigration Commission), *Emigration Conditions in Europe* (Washington, D.C., 1911), pp. 262-63; Stanley Feldstein, *The Land That I Show You* (Garden City, 1978). pp. 100 ff.; Hans Rogger, "Tsarist Policy on Jewish Emigration," in *Soviet Jewish Affairs*, III, no. 1 (1973), 26 ff. See also Heinz-Dietrich Löwe, *Antisemitismus und reaktionäre Utopie* (Hamburg, 1979).

3. Dubnow, II, 279; Greenberg, II, 57.

4. Jacob Riis, *How the Other Half Lives* (New York, 1895), pp. 104-5.

5. Michael Gold, *Jews Without Money* (New York, 1930), pp. 73-74.

6. Sholom Aleichem (*né* Shalom Rabinowitz), *Tevye's Daughters* (New York, 1949), pp. 57-58; Alfred Kazin, *A Walker in the City* (New York, 1951), pp. 17-18.

7. Alfred Kazin, *New York Jew* (New York, 1978), p. 276.

8. *American Jewish Archives*, XVIII (1966), 137.

9. The following memoirs originally appeared, in a somewhat different format, in the April, 1981, issue of *American Jewish Archives*. I was the Guest Editor for that issue. I am grateful to the editors of the journal for giving me permission to use the memoirs for inclusion in this book.

Engraving of the expulsion of Jews from a village in Podosk, Russia
(Leslie's Illustrated Newspaper, 1882)

Workers on the Land

Harris Rubin

Jn 1881 after the first pogroms in Russia there was a large emigration from Russia to America. There was also a strong movement for [agricultural] colonization in America which was strongly supported by the [Viennese] Hebrew journal *Hashahar*. There grew in me a burning desire to go to America. The desire was there, no means of fulfillment. In Southern Russia [the Ukraine], the area of the pogroms, societies were organized for the purpose of facilitating emigration to America for farming, one society being Am Olam, the eternal people.

In our area, Lithuania, since there had been no pogroms there was no effort to organize emigration. So the only means available to me was to write letters to various committees in the towns where emigration was taking place and whose names and addresses I found in the Hebrew journals. These committees wrote me polite replies, but advised me to remain where I was. But soon some people in our area began to talk about America.

At the end of the summer of 1881 my brother-in-law Rosen who lived in Panavezsh came to my *shtetl* [village] Kavarsk on a visit and brought with him a letter from his brother-in-law Goldshtick, now known by the name of LeMaire. Goldshtick gave a glowing description of the welcome he had received in America. A few weeks later we learned that Rosen himself, alone, had gone to America. Of course this only increased our desire to go to the Golden Land. But desire is all that came of it for the very plain and simple reason that I did not have the small number of rubles needed for the journey.

At the beginning of 1882 a letter arrived in Vilkomir from a Mr. Silberman, who had been in New York for two years. In this letter he extolled the material benefits for Jewish immigrants in America to such an extent that the whole town was talking about it. When that letter reached my mother-in-law, of blessed memory, she immediately brought it to me in Kavarsk.

I must at this point remark that my mother-in-law was punctiliously pious and observant and she had strong misgivings about my remaining true to God and her daughter were I to go to profligate America. However, she had such confidence in me that not only did she herself bring the letter but she also persuaded my wife not to oppose me in this matter. I have never forgotten this effort which she made and the confidence she had in me. It was always a source of deep regret to me that I caused her suffering in later years because I was only true to her confidence in me with respect to being true to her daughter, not with respect to being true to God.

The letter which she brought brought matters to a climax. I arrived at such a level of enthusiasm that I resolved that, come what may, I would go to America. My plan was to arrange passage just to London so I could leave a few rubles for my wife, hoping that when I arrived in London I would not be sent back.

On the first month of Adar about six weeks before Passover at 1 p.m., I finished teaching my last pupil and said to them all, "Now you are free from further schooling until you get another teacher because I am going to America." There was big commotion in the *shtetl* because of my announcement. The parents of the pupils complained over the fact that I had not completed the term, but I convinced them that I was really doing them a favor. I promised them that I would write them the truth about conditions in America so they could make proper arrangements for emigrating because in truth everyone was beginning to think about going to America. And so I managed to placate them.

I began to "gather" for the journey. This gathering had nothing to do with packing my trunks because all my baggage could fit under my arm. The gathering had to do with gathering the few rubles needed to make the trip.

At this point I could mention with praise a person who belonged to a nation concerning which my blood boils with rage, Poland. This was the time when the murderous Poles with atrocious cruelty spilled the blood of Jews in outrageous fashion. This person was the landlord of the *shtetl,* a Pole whose name was Sesitsky and who conducted himself in an exceptional manner. Some people thought he was a little crazy, but if all the Poles were as crazy as he then our brothers in Europe would not have been cruelly slaughtered. Other landlords especially thought he was crazy because he did not go to church and because he took an interest in the Jews of the *shtetl*. For instance, if some misfortune occurred to a Jew in the *shtetl,* this Sesitsky would try to help. At Passover he would send potatoes and money to the poor and needy Jews. If two Jews had a dispute, they would come to him to settle it.

So the idea came to me that perhaps Sesitsky might lend me the few rubles I needed for my trip. I arranged to have a letter written in Polish and I brought it to him. He read it with interest and then he really opened up and gave me a lecture. How did I dare to leave my wife and children to go to the other end of the world? And how did I have the effrontery to think that he would help me in such an unjust project? I let him finish his tirade. Then I spoke my piece and calmed him down. But he flatly refused to give me any help. Well, I thought to myself, he wasn't crazy enough to help me so I'll have to do it without his help.

Two days later a special messenger came suggesting I call on Sesitsky. I lost no time in getting to him. He said, "I've made inquiries about you and people speak well of you. I know I can't dissuade you from going so I'll wish you good fortune on your trip. But I will help your wife. I will let her be a buyer for me of various articles which I will need in my various businesses so she will be able to earn a living." I was very happy about this and felt that this was even better than if he had merely loaned me money for the trip. Not only did I thank him then, but even now we thankfully mention his name because of the support he gave my wife until I was able to send for her. When I gathered enough to get started on my trip, my parents, my friends, and the rabbi of the *shtetl* who gave me a letter of recommendation to the Kovner Rav, Yitzhak Elhanan [Spektor], gathered in my house. With tear filled eyes I tore myself from the arms of my wife and parents and with my pack under my arm I was off to America.

In Kovno [Kaunas], I presented my letter to the Rav, Yitzhak Elhanan. He wrote a postscript to the letter which was quite helpful later on. On my trip I stopped in Koenigsberg and Berlin and I arrived in London at the time of Purim. In London I was hoping to acquire a ship's ticket (*shifskarte*) from the Help Committee because I no longer had enough money to buy a ticket. When I arrived at the Committee's place, I found a large hall containing long benches occupied by Jewish men and women of various ages and various appearances. An angry looking man told me where to sit. After a long wait I was told to enter another room where the Committee sat. I answered their questions and when they learned I was from the Kovner district they were amazed because there had not been any pogroms there. However, I was helped by the fact that I had told them I was a farmer because they were most anxious to give assistance to farmers. I was also helped by the letter of my rabbi which had a postscript signed by Rabbi Yitzhak Elhanan. I had very wisely arranged that the letter made no mention of the fact that my last occupation was teacher.

After they had read the letter carefully they seemed to be much more friendly and I was in their office a longer time than the other applicants. Also they were interested in hearing my reports about the condition of the Russian Jews. Finally they gave me a card which indicated where I should report in two days. I would be listed then for emigration on the next ship and would receive money to sustain me until the date of sailing.

After the two days passed, I reported to the place and there found a long hall where there was a long line of gloomy faces among whom were some of more attractive appearance and some young apparently intelligent people. There were benches all around the hall occupied by women and bundles and children of various ages and many howling babies. The hall was filled with a frightful noise and clamor. The threats of a man that he would expel the noise makers had as much effect as applying leeches to a corpse. This man placed me in a line which continued to grow longer. After a long wait I arrived at the window and presented my card to the man stationed there. After he examined the card he spoke sharply saying, "Your card indicates that you are married and that you have left your family behind. We can't give you preference over whole families who have been waiting a long time and who have priority over you. And above all people like you who left their families behind should not be eligible at all." When I tried to talk to him he said, "I have no time to argue with you"—without even looking at me. I had to leave the window downcast and with a heavy heart, knowing that my few shillings would soon be all gone.

I began to think that perhaps I should remain in London. I decided to consult a countryman whose address I had. Maybe he could find some kind of opening for me in London. He was quite friendly and said, "Don't worry. People do manage to make a living in London." He began to explain various plans which I could consider. Several days went by, however, and I had not connected with anything. I learned that a transport would soon be leaving with emigrants. Since I had plenty of time on my hands I decided that I had nothing to lose by again trying to get on that transport. I presented myself at the same window where I had been so rudely dismissed. The same man was at the window. He asked me a few questions, acting as though he had never seen me before, and in a couple of minutes gave me a card directing me to the first office I had visited. There they gave me enough money to tide me over until the sailing date and told me to report to another office where I would get details about the ship's departure.

The day for all the emigrants to assemble arrived. There we were informed that, since the ship was to sail on a Saturday, in order not to desecrate the Sabbath we were to remain in our lodgings on Friday when we were to be picked up. Money was given to us and also clothes, not new but good, when needed.

So on Friday March 19, 1882, wagons went from one lodging house to another in the Jewish area picking up emigrants until each wagon was fully loaded with men, women and children. The loaded wagons assembled at one place and then all proceeded to the dock. This parade of wagons was the object of much interest to those who saw them. At the dock we were put on a small vessel which took us to our "regular" ship. At that time I thought that all ships were the same, but later I found out that it was only a freighter which had been procured at a low price for the emigrants. I regret that I have forgotten the name of the ship.

The next morning there was a big commotion. Thousands of people, men, women and children, rich and poor, came to visit the ship. At first we thought they had come to see us poor Jewish immigrants about whom the London press had written with great sympathy. But later we found out that they had come to see their beloved elephant Jumbo, who had been bought by Barnum from the London Zoo and with whom we had the honor of sharing the ship.

There were some visitors who really had come to see the Jewish emigrants. Among them was a Christian lady, reputed to be a millionairess, who had donated a great deal of money to the emigrant fund. In her honor we arranged ourselves in a semi-circle and she, together with her entourage, walked past us. Whenever she walked by a woman holding an infant, she would take the infant's hand in hers and say something which of course we did not understand. After this procedure a man gave us a short talk in Yiddish. He gave us rules for our conduct on the ship and also told us that we need have no hesitation about eating meat on the ship because it was kosher. He also told us that matzos [unleavened bread] had been provided. We were sailing ten days before Passover. Finally he introduced us to the *mashgiach,* the supervisor of dietary laws, who would see to it that all food would comply with dietary laws and who would also be our adviser for the entire trip. Following this, we descended into the ship and each one of us received a stack of straw, a quilt and a dipper for water. The women were taken to one "stateroom," the men to another. On the walls were shelves, one above another, with barely enough room for a person to squeeze in. These were to be our beds.

Passage to the New World

On Saturday, March 20th, shortly after noon our ship began to move out of the port. The weather was good and as long as daylight remained we remained on deck and looked at the sights on shore. We continued on deck as darkness fell and watched the flickering lights until we were in the open sea when all we saw was the black water and the stars above. Some of the passengers began to feel seasick and went down to their bunks where they thought they would be more comfortable. But I remained with others on deck until late in the night.

In the middle of the night, when I was already lying down in my lair but not yet asleep, something seemed to drop from above accompanied by a scream, "Help, save me!" "What's the matter?" I asked. Came the answer, "I feel very sick. A little water, I'm dying." I got off my shelf with the greatest caution because I didn't want to be hit by contents of the stomach being steadily disgorged by my upper neighbor. When I got up and walked by the women's quarters, I heard more screaming. Other men were up to help the sick. In a little while our whole stateroom was filled with sick and "nurses." There was a running to the sailors for water and to the doctor for help and medicine. Instead of water and medicine we received a bawling out for having disturbed their sleep. There was not sleep for any of the

Praying en route

passengers for the rest of the night.

For the next couple of days those who first became seasick did recover and then others became sick. I was among these. During the period of seasickness no one was at all interested in eating. When we had recovered from being seasick we had the desire to fill our stomachs but nothing to fill them with. It was not because there was any lack of quantity. The tables were loaded with bread, butter, herring, cake and potatoes in their skins and we were free to take as much as we wished. But the trouble was that we could not put the stuff in our mouths. The butter smelled like old wax, the herring like raw fresh fish. The cake was moldy. The bread and potatoes without good reason had a nauseating taste.

As for the so called kosher meat, hardly anyone touched it, some because of their strict observance of dietary laws and some because it made them sick. That meat was about as kosher as I am 25 years old. One of our group had gone into the kitchen and discovered that our so called kosher meat was not ritually salted and was prepared in the same pots and pans as the non-kosher meat. When we complained to the *mashgiach* that this type of procedure rendered the meat non-kosher he blithely said it was sufficient that a ritual slaughterer had certified the meat kosher. So we no longer paid any attention to the *mashgiach* and survived on bread, potatoes and black coffee. Actually no one was too concerned about food.

The first week of the trip was quite pleasant. We spent most of the time on the deck looking at the sea and talking about America. The most pleasant day was the eighth day of our trip, the sabbath, beginning in the morning.

The incident I am about to relate had a comical aspect but I'm telling it because it had a tragic aspect. My purpose is to show what our German brethren really thought of us. They held us in such low esteem and considered us so ignorant that they had picked out one of their esteemed persons to be our teacher on the trip, a person who in truth was not worthy to polish the boots of the lowest of our group.

And now to the story. Early Sabbath morning our *mashgiach* appeared. We had not seen him for several days and had not wanted to see him. He said to us, "Today we shall gather for God's service and I shall preach something worthwhile to you." All of us naturally greeted these words by exchanging smiles. But before we could reply he left our stateroom. The pious ones of our group decided that if he really returned they would let him know just what they thought of him. But we all agreed we would let him preach and have a little fun at his expense.

In a little while he returned with candles in one hand and candlesticks in the other. "Now let's assemble for God's service. I will serve as your cantor," he said. At that point, when we realized that this fellow was so ignorant of our religious practice that he did not know it was improper to kindle any kind of fire on the sabbath, the pious ones could not restrain themselves and berated him and told him that if he did not leave immediately he would be physically attacked. This fellow had the unmitigated gall to insult the Russian Jews. It became such a scandalous situation that the captain heard about it.

When the captain entered the stateroom, this *mashgiach* fellow immediately addressed him and described us as if we were the worst criminals. Luckily for us, some of our emigrants understood English and explained to the captain that the *mashgiach* wanted to preach to us after he had done something forbidden by our religion and that when we told him we didn't want any of his preaching he insulted us. Hearing this, the captain grabbed this fellow by the collar and led him out of the stateroom with the strict order never again to enter our stateroom. Later we found out that the captain's friendliness to us was in his own interest. When we were approaching New York, the captain asked us to sign a paper saying that we had received only the best treatment on the ship. Regardless of the reason for his friendliness, we had bested the *mashgiach* and we had a very warm and pleasant sabbath morning. As the weather was splendid we were in good spirits.

The afternoon of that sabbath day was interesting. It had to do with the maneuver which the captain conducted with the sailors as required on each trip. At a signal the sailors came arunning, some stationing themselves at the masts at the sail ropes, some at the lifeboats. At another signal some climbed the masts, some climbed into the life boats which were lowered into the water. While we were feeling entertained by all this, at the same time we were a bit frightened because it meant the captain was expecting bad weather. And that is what happened. During the life boat drill the weather was gorgeous, but the next morning, Sunday, the sea began to get rough. By the afternoon the storm arrived. The whole sea was an expanse of mountainous waves and the ship was battered about like a splinter up one wave and down another and the storm continued to worsen.

Sunday evening we were warned not to come on deck. In our stateroom we were not able to stand or sit and if we attempted to lie down in our bunks we were shaken out. Trunks, benches and other objects slid from one side of the ship to the other. Monday morning when some of us wanted to poke our heads out of the door leading to the deck it was frightening to see the huge waves black as ink which appeared ready to swallow the entire ship. Everything on deck was covered with ice. The raincoats worn by the sailors on deck seemed to be made of tin because of the freezing. Everyone in our quarters was very frightened, especially the Jews. The women were crying. The men gathered together and were reciting psalms.

When night came the storm became more violent. We had agreed to conduct a *seder* service because it was the eve of Passover but we were unable to do it. The *knaidlich* [dumplings], the four cups of wine, the *charoseth* [special Passover salad], even the matzoh which the Committee had provided, we were not able to enjoy. We did however manage to read the *Haggadah* [Passover exodus narrative] and the *Hallel* [holiday psalms] hoping thereby to receive the favor of God by whose mercy we might be saved from the threatening danger. There were, however, some women who had taken tablecloths from their suitcases and spread them over some tables, and on these tables portion of matzoh were placed. Some better families had brought their own matzoh, wine and Passover whiskey and these were placed on the tables. But everything placed on the tables had to be securely held by someone.

We sat around the tables holding onto the table and the bench. One of the men who had brought his own wine recited the *Kiddush* [sanctification over wine] and the blessing over matzoh. There was a father whose son asked the four questions. The Four Questions and the recitation of "This is the bread of affliction" were about as appropriate to our situation as the furs worn by our women on a hot summer day. But just as our women do it to serve fashion, so we felt duty bound to serve God whether it was appropriate or not. When we reached the point in the *Haggadah* of reciting the *Hallel* psalms, there was such an alarm and such loud crying by the women that the non-Jewish passengers, the sailors, and even the captain came running to our quarters. No one, however, interfered with us. As a matter of fact, the captain was quite pleased.

When we finished the *Hallel* and our trouble-filled *seder* service, we had some short conversations. Their theme was that if we wanted God to save us we had to decide then and there that we would not forget God and his Torah when we arrived in profligate America. After this, we ate some of the dry *matzoh*, which we were barely able to swallow because it was so dry. It must have been baked when the Jews made the Exodus from Egypt. It was now late in the night and the storm still continued. Now tired, hungry and sleepy, we crawled into our bunks. But sleep wasn't possible. Every time the ship rolled we thought it was going to completely turn over. The women were crying. The men were trying to comfort them. And if this were not enough, one of the passengers gave us such a scare that it's a wonder our souls remained in our bodies.

About three o'clock in the morning we were aroused by loud screams from an upper deck. Half dead, half alive and only partly dressed, we all ran to the upper deck from where the screams came. "What's the matter? What happened?" we asked the man from whom the screams emanated. "You're asking what's the matter," he said. "Don't you realize the storm is worse? Don't you know one of the masts has been broken? How can you sleep in such a situation?" We answered, "What can we do?" And he replied "Recite psalms!" Naturally we were quite angry at this fellow and the Christians were ready to lynch him. But we already had had our sleep interrupted. So we really did recite psalms. And we did it with such fervor and weeping that we awakened all the ship's passengers. The Christians protested vigorously because we had disturbed them and they complained to the captain. When he heard the whole story he upbraided them for interfering with us. "They are praying to God for you as well as themselves," he said, "and instead of being grateful to them you are laughing at them and disturbing them because you're losing a few hours sleep." To us he expressed the hope and expectation that the storm would abate the next day. The next morning the storm decreased and in the afternoon the weather was pleasant. So it remained until we arrived in New York.

After the stormy weather had ended, a stronger storm arose in our bellies. Our appetites grew very strong but we had nothing with which to satisfy them because only a little while ago we had promised God to be pious and since we believed that God stilled the storm because of our promise, most of us would not eat any *chometz,* food not ritually fit for the eight days of Passover.

So from Monday evening until Friday we survived on a few pieces of *matzoh* which we received twice a day, which we would not have eaten if we had not been so hungry, and some potatoes that had been steamed in their skins. By Friday all the *matzoh* had been consumed, so Friday evening dinner and Saturday morning breakfast consisted of *matzoh* crumbs and for the rest of Saturday we had only potatoes. And since the very pious did not eat the potatoes they in fact fasted that day. But we didn't feel too hungry that day because we were told that we were to arrive in New York that day. In the afternoon we saw land and we were no longer thinking about eating. On Saturday evening we stopped a short distance from the port and on Sunday, April 4th, on the eve of the last day of Passover, a smaller ship took us to Castle Garden.

Is This Really America?

When we sailed from London, the London Committee told us that a committee would meet us in New York and take care of our needs. During the whole trip we anticipated the grand reception we were to receive. Some of us fantasized that we would be welcomed with music. But after we had finished with all the necessary procedures for entrance into our new country and had gone through the last door one at a time, we looked here and there and everywhere hoping to see the committee but there was not even a trace of it. Well the music and even the grand reception we could do without. But would that they had brought something to still our hunger! They should have realized that since it was Passover we would not eat *chometz.* "But go talk to the wall." There was no one there to talk to. The only people who were of some help to us were the people who had come to welcome relatives among our group of emigrants. These people helped change our German and English money into American money so that we were able to buy some apples to still our hunger. They were also helpful in escorting us to the Jewish quarter where we would be able to either eat in a kosher restaurant or buy something to eat.

I didn't go with that group. I agreed to watch their baggage while they went to eat, and they promised to return with food for me. But it was four hours before they returned because they lost their way back to Castle Garden. I was ravenously hungry by that time and before they finished telling me of their difficulty in finding their way back to me I had the bundle of food in my hands. My eyes really lit up when I saw good *matzoh*, not like the ship's, salami and fruit, enough to provide two meals for three. But before I had taken the first bite I was surrounded by hungry women and children with tears in their eyes begging for some morsels to still their hunger. So I shared my bundle of food with them so that we each had only a couple of mouthfuls. We all were still hungry while we continued to wait for the committee.

Night was approaching, our strength was waning because of hunger, the committee had not appeared, so we hit on this plan. We would send a few of our bold young men to the Jewish quarter where they would locate a synagogue where Jews would be gathering for the evening prayers and there the young men would raise a hue and cry about our situation. The young men did an excellent job. When they arrived in the Jewish quarter they got directions to the largest Orthodox synagogue (if I'm not mistaken, it was the Kalverier synagogue) and they arrived as the synagogue was nearly filled with people about to begin the evening service. But before the cantor reached the pulpit our young men shouted, "You dear Jews are about to chant the evening service and then you will return to your homes for your holiday meal. But in Castle Garden there are several hundred Jews who have had almost nothing to eat for two days and if you don't do something about it they are going to be forced to eat *chometz*."

There was then an uproar in the synagogue. The evening service was postponed. A *matzoh* baker was ordered to immediately send 200 pounds of *matzohs* to Castle Garden and some of the people went around to certain homes collecting food. Before our young men had returned to give us their report, a wagon arrived with a huge case of *matzoh*. In a few minutes that case was opened and surrounded by people who fell on it like locusts. There was pushing and shoving until the group who had brought the *matzoh* assured everyone that there was enough for everyone. Actually there was more than enough for everyone, including some Christians who joined us.

By the time we had filled our bellies with dry matzoh, a group of well dressed Jews appeared carrying heavy baskets which were filled with good things, meat, chickens, Passover cake, wine and whiskey. Then it was "To the Jews" and all of us partook of the goodies. Then we had a little whiskey. Everything seemed friendly and orderly. We forgot our troubles. We felt the Jews were different than the other nations and we felt that America was different than the land we had left. The men who had brought baskets of food spent a couple of hours with us in pleasant conversation and then told us that a few of them would come the next morning and escort all our men to the synagogue services after which each synagogue member would take one of us to his home for the midday meal and all the meals for the two last days of the Passover holiday. At first we refused because we felt we were lowering ourselves to accept. But these men were persistent in a friendly manner and they told us we should not feel like hodge podge beggars but like invited guests. And each one of us was formally invited with the words "I desire that you be my guest." So naturally we accepted this very friendly invitation.

Monday morning a few men came, lined us up in pairs and marched us to the synagogue. It would be superfluous for me to describe the Americans who stopped to watch us as we marched. We received a very friendly reception when we arrived at the synagogue and after the service each one of us was invited by a member to be his guest. There were more hosts than guests and the hosts who had no guests seemed to be disappointed. The women and children who had been left at Castle Garden were a bit disappointed, but arrangements were made so that they had their fill of food. We had to return to Castle Garden for sleeping and there we slept like lords on the bare, dirty stone floor. To sleep in Castle Garden was a privilege given only to Jewish immigrants.

During these last two days of the Passover holiday I sought out some countrymen whose addresses I had. Some advised that I forget about the committee and become a peddler as many earlier immigrants had done. Others advised that I wait and see what the committee could do for me and if that were not satisfactory then I could become a peddler. I accepted the second idea.

The two days went by and no committee appeared. Some of the immigrants decided not to wait for the committee and went out on their own to seek employment. But I and a number of others hung around Castle Garden. Finally, on the fifth day, some people appeared and took us to the "regular immigrant house" in Green Point. While it was true that this immigrant house provided warm cooked meals at tables and real beds for sleeping, in some respects it was less desirable than Castle Garden. The beds were dirty and filled with little creatures which tormented the soldiers in the trenches. The discipline was militaristic and the man in charge was an angry old German Jew, the same type as the *mashgiach* on the ship. If one of us wanted to go somewhere or even write a letter, it was necessary to get permission from that despot.

Every day ten or twelve of us were selected, dressed in white uniforms, and given the job of washing dishes, cleaning beds and so on. The food was of the cheapest grade. It was a paradox to compare this situation with the reception given to us by our fellow Jews in the synagogue. In a sense it was natural that there be a difference. In the synagogue the Jews were plain folk like us who had felt the Russian whip and the bitter taste of being immigrants, and they empathized with us. On the other hand, in this immigrant house we were dealing with a committee of an organization run by German Jews who did not have too much love for Russian Jews but provided help out of a cold sense of philanthropy, and therefore the system and discipline which resulted were suited to uncivilized recipients which they considered us to be.

In addition to operating Immigrant House, the committee operated an employment bureau for jobs in the country as well as the city. On our second day at Immigrant House I and some others went to the employment bureau. Those who had a trade were given jobs in their trade, others were given labor work if it were available. I listed my work as farmer and they told me that they were especially anxious to help one who wanted to be a farmer, that I would first have to work with an American farmer to learn the American system of farming which was quite different from the Russian, and that I would be notified as soon as they arranged for me to be placed with a farmer. When I asked about pay they told me I would get between 12 and 15 dollars a month. This was 24 to 40 rubles a month, which was much better than I earned as a teacher, and furthermore it also provided bed and board. So, feeling very happy, I returned to the barracks which they called Immigrant House to await their notification.

A few days later Mr. Goldshtick, a countryman whom I've mentioned before, came to see me at Immigrant House. He had already been in America for a year and made his living as a peddler in the rural areas. When I told him that my goal was to be a farmer and that I was awaiting notice from the committee, he tried to dissuade me from this plan. First he pointed out that the work would be arduous and second that I would be put in an area where there were no Jews and I would therefore be unable to observe my religion. I answered that I could do heavy work because I had already done it. As to the religious problem of eating non-kosher food and working on the sabbath, well I was no longer on the stormy sea and no longer afraid and my thoughts and feelings were returning to me. Furthermore, even according to the Talmud itself, I would be allowed to forego some religious practices for a time and God would forgive me because of the high idealistic purpose I had in mind, the idea of Zionism which held that the future of Jewish life demanded that Jews become farmers and colonists.

Goldshtick realized I was not going to change my mind and since he himself was a follower of *haskalah* [i.e., was an emancipated intellectual] he then suggested that I let him, rather than the committee, find a farmer with whom I could live and work because the committee might send me to a non-desirable place or a non-desirable farmer. He had been peddling in the farming areas and would pick for me a good spot and good honest people whom he knew were looking for green hands. He was planning to leave the next day and promised to write me as soon as he found a good spot. Within two days I got a letter saying he had found a good place. He gave clear and detailed instructions for my trip to Albany where I was to meet him in a certain boarding house on a Saturday.

If I had had the money for my expenses for an Albany trip, I would have left immediately since it was on Friday that I had received Goldshtick's letter. Not having the money, I tried to get it at the employment bureau. They at first refused on the ground that they did not approve of acting on the advice of one individual unknown to them. At that point I made the threat that if they would not give me the money I would abandon the idea of working for a farmer. They said they'd give me the money if I could give them some references about my friend Goldshtick. By the time I was able to get these references from my countrymen, it was already Saturday. It was Saturday evening by the time they gave me a two dollar bill and a ticket to Albany on an immigrant train which took all night, so I arrived in Albany Sunday morning. I went to Goldshtick's boarding house and learned that he had left on Saturday leaving no word for me other than telling them that a "greenie" might come there for him. I stayed there all day and lodged there that night but he did not appear.

Not Wisdom but Chutzpah

Monday morning, having paid for board and lodging, I didn't have enough for a return ticket to New York or even to remain in Albany another night. Goldshtick's letter had named the various stops which the train would have to make when we would leave Albany for his farmer's place. So having no other course open I got on that train hoping that at one of the stops I would by some miracle meet him. At the first stop, which I think was Louisville, I got off carrying my suitcase and asked for the hotel (luckily the same word in Yiddish as in English) which was near the depot. When I arrived there, my total vocabulary was three words, peddler, Goldshtick, farmer. The crowd at the hotel didn't understand so they fetched a German who managed to understand me somewhat and told me that he had seen Goldshtick on Saturday afternoon.

So I went to the next stop. Alas no Goldshtick. So I went to the third and last stop, Devensburg, from which it was, according to the letter, four miles to the farm. When I got off that train and looked around, I felt sure Goldshtick had made a mistake. He had described this third stop as a railroad station (naturally, he had no other word to call it), but all I saw was what might be described as a small wooden shed and two men, one wearing overalls over a pair of pants, the other wearing an old worn out coat sitting at a noise-making telegraph apparatus who seemed to be the station master. I addressed him with my monologue, peddler, Goldshtick, farmer. He smiled, said some words I didn't understand except that I recognized the words wife and house as he pointed to a nearby house. There the woman recognized the name Goldshtick but was of no further help. Goldshtick's letter indicated that nearby was the village of Devensburg, which had a hotel. I left my bag at the station and went to the hotel. There I saw a number of men sitting on the porch with their feet raised to the railing and chewing continuously. I later learned that in America men chewed tobacco. From their stares it was clear to me that I seemed to them some kind of strange creature. I addressed them with my three word speech. There were smiles and some words I didn't understand. I went across the street to a store with the same result. My heart was filled with pain. No Goldshtick. No farmer. No money. Fifty-three cents left. I was as hungry as fifteen wolves. I began to be seriously concerned and I concluded that it had really been a crazy idea to expect a miracle to solve my problem.

But actually a small miracle did occur. In my bewilderment I did something which in normal circumstances would be considered sheer lunacy. I stopped every single person passing through the village addressing him with my three words even though I realized how hopeless it all seemed to be. And yet this foolish procedure brought better results than some brilliant ideas. Late in the afternoon, when I was about to give up in despair, there approached a beautiful pair of horses mounted by two men who appeared to be father and son. I approached them and said "Peddler, Goldshtick," and before I got to the third word they shouted, "Yes, yes!" You can imagine how relieved I was to have found the farmer. It seemed to me at that time to be the finger of God. Today I realize it was not wisdom but chutzpah to think that God would take the time from his care of millions of unlucky folks all over the world to direct his attention to just one person and put the idea into the mind of a farmer in this remote place to appear at this moment to meet me so I would not be forced to spend the night on the bare earth. But at that time my understanding was different. (Today I think my former ideas about God to be absurd. And yet I know that 99 percent of people, including many very learned people, hold fast to these ideas which I have discarded. I realize I have wandered from my story but whenever I compare my former ideas, which are still held by most people, and my present thinking. I have a weakness for wanting to talk about it. But now I'll go back to my story.)

After the farmer and I had rejoiced over meeting each other, the first thing he did was to lead me into the hotel and treat me to a drink, which was a great relief to my hunger. It was a great regret to me that following the example of the farmer I only poured half a glass for myself. Just in passing I must point out that here I saw a difference between the Russian peasant and the American. In the homeland when a peasant ordered a drink in an inn, his glass was always filled to overflowing, but here in this country the peasant (well isn't a farmer a peasant?) who ordered a drink poured it himself and only half filled the glass. (Later I learned that the American farmer in some respects had a higher standing than a landlord in my old homeland.) The whiskey made me feel more cheerful and I forgot my recent difficulties. The farmer's son accompanied me to the depot to pick up my box, a new word which I added to my vocabulary, and so the farmer and his son headed for home with their great find, me.

When we reached their farmhouse the farmer's son jumped off the wagon and told the family that the new hand recommended by the peddler Goldshtick had arrived. The whole family came out to look me over. I'm sure I did not make a favorable impression with my long coat reaching below my knees and my pale cheeks. But they gave no visible expression of their disappointment. To the contrary, the whole family gave me a very warm welcome and tried to talk to me. I looked in their eyes or around them and just shook my head. When they realized what kind of a creature they had to deal with, they used sign language to invite me into the house.

I was astounded by the cleanliness and tidiness of the room. I was equally astounded when I was led to the room where I was to leave my small suitcase which I understood to be my room. There I saw a clean bed covered with a bedspread and several fine pieces of furniture. And I am not ashamed to say that until then I had never seen so clean and attractive a room except for the rooms I had seen in the czar's palace in Gatchina.

When I came downstairs the farmer said something to his wife and she immediately set on the table, which was covered with a white tablecloth, a plate of sliced bread, butter, preserves, cake and pie. They indicated I should sit and eat. Although I felt a little awkward for the first time sitting at a non-Jewish table (no meat was on the table), I didn't wait for a second invitation. In a few minutes I cleaned up what had been put on the table. Even today it is a source of wonderment to me that they didn't put me in the wagon and send me back because later I found out that what I had eaten was enough to feed the whole family for one meal.

After I had eaten they asked about my name. I answered Harris Rubin which was the name the committee had assigned me. They all said it was a pretty name, but now I know that they would have said that no matter what the name. Knowing my name, the farmer said, "Come on, Harris," and giving me a wink made me understand that I was to follow him. I followed him into a shed filled with farming implements where the young man with whom I recently arrived was working. But I hardly recognized him because he was wearing an odd old yellow costume, overalls and jumper, and wearing a wide straw hat. The old farmer dressed himself in a similar costume and said something to the young man, who then handed me a similar but old discarded uniform, and without any further advice I put it on. When I observed my appearance in a small mirror it was a shock and I could not help wondering what my former pupils would have thought had they seen me so attired.

When I was ready, they led me into the stable and the first honor they gave me was to clean up the stable where the cows stood. This did not appeal too much to me, especially did it not appeal to my sense of smell, but there is a saying, "If you are a soldier you have to smell gunpowder," so I decided that if I wanted to be a farmer I would have to smell something that smelled worse than gunpowder. So I went to it and when I finished they gave me some other work which did not smell so bad.

At five o'clock the farmer made the motion of putting his finger in his mouth. I didn't know what this meant but I noticed that they put their tools down so I did the same. They walked to the house so I followed them. They took off their costumes and washed, so then I understood the meaning of putting the fingers to the mouth, "let's eat." I followed their actions. I took off my costume, I washed, I combed my hair as they did. But I wanted to beg off when it came to eating because I had just finished eating enough to last twenty-four hours. But they insisted I join them at the table. When I entered the dining room, the farmer's wife appeared dressed up like a lady of the manor. The table was set with beautiful dishes and so many courses that I asked myself, "Is this a peasant's table?" This table was far more attractive than that of a landlord in the Old Country and I thought to myself, "This is America. This is an American farmer." I thought that if I could attain my goal of being an American farmer it would be a thousand times better than I had ever imagined it would be.

I was anxious to write home to tell them of the impression made on me by America and American farming. But while I was engaged in this day dreaming the farmer asked me "Can you milk?" The similarity to Yiddish was such that I understood the question. But I didn't know how to answer. "What kind of work is this for me?" I wondered. I would have to seat myself at cow's rear end and tug on her teats. In the Old Country this was women's work. If I answered that I didn't know how I might lose my job. Again I reminded myself, "If you are a soldier you have to smell gunpowder." All this went through my mind in an instant and when the farmer made sign language about milking, I answered, "Yes."

He took me to a stall after pointing to his two boys, who were already milking. I sat down on a stool, placed the bucket between my feet and proceeded to squeeze the cow's teats. But I was getting almost no results. The farmer was observing my fumbling and I couldn't help but feel that I would be getting my discharge momentarily. But he merely asked me to get up, sat down and in a short time filled the bucket with milk from the same cow. Then we both knew that I knew nothing about milking. I felt very uncomfortable because I had told him I knew how to milk a cow. What he thought, I do not know, but he was friendly and gave me another task while he and his boys finished the milking.

When the milking was finished we provided supper for the cows, the horses and the pigs. And that ended the day's work. Then the work clothes were removed. Everyone washed and this time even the feet were washed and the socks were changed and while some wore slippers, some wore just socks alone, as on the fast day of the Ninth of Ab. All went to the parlor. The man read either a book or newspaper. One of the daughters played the organ. (Pianos had not reached the farmers.) The farmer's wife was busy mending and sewing. And I sat there like a rooster among men. At first they tried to converse with me, but when they found that was like talking to a wall they gave up. I felt uncomfortable sitting there silent like a clumsy fellow. So I went up to my room and picked up a Hebrew book which I had brought with me. I went back to the parlor, sat down and began to read. One of the boys came over to look at the book and immediately there was great interest and curiosity. The book was passed from one to the other and turned from side to side and there was much shrugging of shoulders and an amazement that such a language could be read.

When in answer to their question I told them that the language was

Hebrew, their wonderment increased and they became so elated that the boys went down to the cellar and returned with a pitcher of cider and some beautiful apples. One of the daughters poured the cider into glasses, set them on a tray and served each person. The other daughter put the apples on a tray and served each person also. The cider was an exceptionally good drink. Everyone became a little friendlier, even I. Suddenly there was a knock on the door. All eyes turned. Who would be knocking at such a late hour? It was nearly 10 o'clock and among farmers that is late. When the door was opened, there stood Goldshtick. Everyone was excited and very happy to see him, I even more than the others. It seemed that a new spirit had entered into me.

Goldshtick explained that he had arrived in Devensburg late in the evening and there he was told that a greenie was looking for him and that the greenie had been taken to the farm of the Macmillans. Goldshtick left his peddler's pack at the hotel and in the dark walked the four miles to the farm. That is an example of the great friendship between us. He was tired and hungry, so he was treated to some cider and refreshments and the family celebrated with us until midnight. He shared my bed and we talked most of the night. Nevertheless, I arose at the regular time and performed the tasks assigned to me. At breakfast he gave me some instruction in table manners and named the various courses which were set out on the table and also told the farmer something about me. The farmer told him about the milking incident and they joked about it. The farmer said that he was confident that I would learn and that he needed me especially for the harvest time, which was some months away, and that I would probably learn my job by that time and that he would pay me $15 per month, which was quite satisfactory to me.

After breakfast Goldshtick and I talked awhile and he promised to return to see me in a couple of weeks and then took off to the hotel to pick up his peddler's pack. When he left, I felt forsaken. Here on this farm I was really alone among people to whom my feelings, my character and my psychology were about as far away as East from West, people with whom I could not exchange a word. And when I realized I would be here at least six months, my heart grew so heavy I barely restrained myself from tears. You can therefore imagine how uplifted I felt when Goldshtick returned in about an hour and told me that he had been talking to a farmer who lived in the area. This farmer asked Goldshtick if he could recommend an immigrant who would be as good a worker as I and this farmer was even willing to pay Goldshtick's expenses to and from New York if he could find so good a worker as I. I knew of such an immigrant and gave his name to Goldshtick, who took the next train to New York. The very next day Goldshtick returned with the man, whose name was Schneider. I particularly mention his name because ten years later he played an important role in Newark as a rich Jew and politician.

When they arrived I was as happy as if I had just won a great fortune because now I could at least look forward to some companionship at least once a week, Sunday. Without this I was fearful I would forget how to speak. Every Sunday Schneider and I spent the whole day together. Although he was a plain and ordinary fellow, we felt strongly drawn to each other because not only were we both in the same situation in America, but just as I had left a wife and seven children in the Old Country, he too had left a wife and children there. We each looked forward eagerly to spending Sunday together.

The first Sunday Schneider came to visit me. The second Sunday I went to visit him. There I met another young Jewish farm worker who already spoke English. This young man not only increased the size of our group but he taught us English and acted as our interpreter whenever necessary. We asked him how he had heard of us and he told us that the whole area was talking of the fact that Macmillan and Kuns (Schneider's boss) had hired Jewish farm hands.

In order to explain how news of every little happening on a farm would spread for miles around, I want to report two incidents. I noticed that an American cat would mew the same as Russian cat, so I said that the American cat could speak Russian. This story spread all around the area and wherever I went I was pointed out as having said it. Another time when I was driving a pair of horses and brought them to a stop by yelling, as in Lithuania, "Tprrru"— this was imitated and discussed whenever local farmers got together.

The third Sunday we went to visit our new comrade four miles from me and so we continued to meet each Sunday at one of the three farms and all three of us would dine with the family at whose farm we were meeting. Goldshtick arranged his schedule so that he would join us every fourth Sunday at Macmillan's. So that made four Jews meeting at one time and we made a regular holiday out of it.

In spite of these pleasant respites, it took an iron patience to hold out for the whole summer. I must say that I had a good job, good board and good treatment. However, I did suffer greatly in the realization that I was only a farm hand and also that in one stroke I had torn myself from my former strong Jewish roots. This was a torment, a suffering of the spirit. But I also suffered physically. Previously I said that I was freed of the job of milking, but this was only a temporary freedom. When the work of the farm increased I was given a broad hint that I should learn milking so I proceeded to the task, but my fingers, the fingers which had done only teacher's work, weren't suited to milking a cow and they hurt, the fingers, and perhaps also the teats of the cow. Every morning my fingers were sore and swollen and when I would herd the cows for the milking I would be constantly flexing my fingers to try to get them in shape to do the milking. Finally, the pain was such that I could no longer do any milking, which was not accepted in good grace by the farmer. But I was greatly relieved when I was freed of that task and put to work carrying the milk to the cellar and properly storing it there. I was put in charge of this operation and I treated myself well with milk and cream.

In mid-July harvesting hay began and so did hard times for me. Whoever has been involved in this knows how arduous it is, especially when a cloud appears while the dry cut hay is on the fields. The hay harvesting lasts four to six weeks in this area. It is their main crop. It is immediately followed by the grain harvest. It was just too much for me. First because I was not used to such continuous hard physical labor and secondly because the use of farm machinery produced as much work in a day as was done in Russia in a week.

Here is a specific instance of this situation. Once, when there was much hay lying waiting to be hauled away, heavy clouds appeared. Immediately there was a great deal of hustle and bustle to get the hay in the loft before the rain fell. I was given the honor of working in the loft stacking the hay as it came off the machine which brought it up a couple of hundred pounds at a time. This work itself was very strenuous. The heat under the roof of that barn plus the heat which came from the hay itself was simply unbearable and the close quarters compounded the hardships. I was very tired and could not handle the machine to suit one of the farmer's boys, who ran up to take over from me and honored me with an American curse. I honored him with a louder voicing of a Russian curse. He was so surprised that he stood looking at me open mouthed. I don't know whether it was the Russian curse or the anger in my eyes which stunned him. I didn't want to work anymore. His father came arunning to placate me. I let myself be persuaded and our angers subsided, but our friendship after that was different.

Toward the end of the harvest I was again given the job of storing oats in the loft. It was an unusually hot day. That night as I sat at the supper table the chair and the area around the chair were wet with my sweat. The next morning the pain in my back was so great I barely got out of bed. I went to the stable to pitch some hay to feed the cows and I fell down in a faint. I was carried into my bed where I remained for several days. It was then that I really got a taste of loneliness. I was so weak and helpless that they had to undress me. They had to carry my food up to me. I felt unwelcomed. As soon as I was able to get on my feet I requested that they pay me the wages due me and take me to the station so that I could return to New York. Since I couldn't do any more work and since the busy season was over, they complied with my request.

While I was waiting at the station for the New York train, it occurred to me that I would be arriving in New York about the time of the High Holidays, and I would not be able to do any work and the little bit of money I had would be all gone. So I decided to take the train to a nearby village where Goldshtick had his headquarters and that I would then talk things over with him. My two other Jewish farm workers and I had spent the 4th of July there as guests of Goldshtick at a holiday dinner and celebration which he hosted.

Goldshtick was not there when I arrived. The lady of the house where we had the dinner remembered me. I told her I was sick, unable to work. She suggested that I remain in her house for a few days to recuperate and that if I wished I could work for her when I was physically able and that if I was not recovered in four or five days she would not charge me anything. This suited me fine so I remained. Her husband and she were an elderly couple. He was unable to work. While she was old, she was healthy and still able to manage their small farm nearby and this very substantial house in which I stayed with them. She took good care of me and in three days I was able to do a little work. At that time Goldshtick arrived. He suggested that I remain at this house for about a month which would bring us to the Succoth fall harvest holidays and that I could then return to New York.

When my two comrades learned that I had not yet gone to New York they came to visit me and agreed to join me on my trip to New York. Although my job was an easy one, my board was first class and my employers treated me well, I began to count the minutes until I would leave for New York. Although I had to wait only a month it seemed like a year. When the happy day arrived, my two comrades and Goldshtick joined me and together we left for New York. This ended the first chapter of my American career.

Beginning the American Dream

At the time when I was still working for farmer Macmillan, Goldshtick told me that my plan to become a farmer was impractical. Nevertheless, when I got to New York I sought out the Committee only to learn that it no longer existed. I did, however, learn of a newly organized private group called Agudath Ovedei Adamah, Union of Workers of the Land, consisting of 100 people whose plan was as follows. Each member was to put up a sum of money which would be used to acquire 100 claims in Western states where there was still government land available. Every year ten of the members would be chosen by lot to start as farmers and the remaining members would assist those in getting started so that in ten years all the members of the group would become farmers. The leader of the organization was a Mr. Sobel, a former rabbi, now a *maskil,* a follower of the Enlightenment movement, and a free thinker, who was a good friend of Goldshtick.

On my second day in New York I met Sobel. He was so happy to meet me he almost kissed me. His married daughter, who had learned midwifery in Russia and who was intelligent and an ardent supporter of the colonization idea and whose husband was a member of the organization, paid me the highest compliments, complimenting me especially on the fact that I had been able to spend six months actually doing hard farm work when most of the immigrants gave up in two weeks. Mr Sobel was so enthusiastic that he promised me that if I joined their group I would be among the first ten to go without being subject to drawing by lot and that they would even forego any deposit of money by me. Nevertheless, I turned it down. After my six months of working on a farm I realized that the members of this group were not really suitable to farming. I also was certain that Jews could not become farmers unless they would be in Jewish surroundings where there would be a synagogue, a *shochet* [ritual slaughterer for kosher meat], a Jewish society, and wives in sympathy with the plan. (I forgot to say previously that Sobel had agreed to bring my family over in order to get me to join up.)

In passing I must report that the plan came to naught. A few groups did go, among them Sobel's daughter, who sent letters of enthusiasm about their new pioneering lives. But as time went on the enthusiasm lessened, the letters began to tell of difficulties and in less than two years they returned to New York to seek some kind of business. I became convinced that I had to give up the idea of becoming a farmer. I had to do something to make a living, so I had to become a peddler as did most of the immigrants.

If I were a skilled writer I would take this opportunity to write at length about the Jewish peddler in America because it was the foundation of the Jewish community in America, the foundation which really saved the Jewish immigrant. The story of the Jewish immigrant would fill a thick book. My circumstances are such that I cannot undertake this task, but I do hope that some capable writer will write that historic episode. I will merely make the following remarks.

In the 1860's when a significant number of Russian-Polish Jews emigrated to America, they were mostly plain, broken down business people or artisans and there were few intellectuals among them. That fact and the fact that except for the German Jews there were no Jewish businesses forced these immigrants into peddling. In the 1880's, after the beginning of the pogroms in Russia when the immigrant numbers were quite high, there were among them many artisans and intellectuals seeking work, but even they mostly went into peddling. Some peddlers worked only in the cities while some worked only in rural areas. The rural or country peddlers were of several kinds. Some sold dry goods, some sold utensils of various kinds, some sold picture frames and jewelry and so on. All of them suffered hardships. The city peddler had to endure the harassment of hoodlums and while the country peddler was free of attacks by hoodlums his work was very arduous. He trudged from one farmhouse to another carrying a heavy pack on his shoulders and until he became known in an area it was difficult for him to find lodging for the night.

There was also a difference in the character of the peddlers. The city peddler had the character of a pure *schnorrer* [sponger]. He would usually have two or three dollars worth of various articles in an open basket which he would display as he went from door to door. People would buy usually out of a feeling of pity for him, and in some cases also because of a need for the articles. The country peddler, on the other hand, had more of a business-like character. He carried a substantial pack of goods and he could and did sell his goods for less than the country store. The results, however, were reversed. The city peddler, if only he had the patience to endure the insults, that is if he could be a good *schnorrer,* would very soon become a customer-peddler, one who had regular customers to whom he sold all of their household needs on installments. Usually in a short time, the city peddler who used to go from house to house with his open basket hanging from his neck would be seen dressed like a sport with a cigar in his mouth and a small briefcase under his arm going from customer to customer taking orders for furniture, clothes or jewelry and collecting for the merchandise previously sold. In a few years the customer-peddler would open a store and sell to new peddlers. The country peddler took longer to get ahead, but most of them did get ahead more or less. In truth, it can be said that most of the Jewish storekeepers in the United States, whether in the city or in the country, got their start as peddlers. Jewish manufacturers arose out of later Jewish immigrants among whom were greater numbers of craftsmen.

Because I was more comfortable in the country than in the city and also because I very much hated anything that smacked of being a *schnorrer,* I decided to be a country peddler as did my comrade Schneider. So right after the [autumnal] Succoth holidays Goldshtick took Schneider and me to a peddler supply house where he opened a credit account of $10 for each of us and with the capital which we already had I acquired $20 worth of stock and Schneider acquired $25 worth of stock. Goldshtick instructed us as to how to pack our stock. He took us on the ferry to New Jersey and put me on the peddler train which ran from Jersey City to Easton on the Central-New Jersey Line. This was called the peddler train because peddlers rode on it without tickets. Goldshtick knew about this and he also knew the area because he had peddled there when he had first arrived in America.

Goldshtick dropped Schneider at the station named White House, about fifty miles from New York. He took me to the fourth station beyond that because he thought that was a better area to peddle and he was friendlier to me than Schneider. There was an iron mine in this area. I should have done better than Schneider, but at the very least I should have done as well, but it turned out otherwise. Schneider immediately began to do well and his business grew from day to day and he became a rich man but I remained a poor peddler. The reason for this was quite simple. I was in my heart still a Yeshiva [talmudic academy] student and an idealist. Schneider had never been a Yeshiva student but he had been a peddler in his youth in the Old Country.

When Goldshtick dropped me at my station I was supposed to go to the first house, ring the bell and show my merchandise. But my heart did not let me do it. The first house looked as though it were occupied by rather well-to-do people who would insult me for bothering them, so I waved my hand at the house and moved on. The next house was quite modest so I thought that poor people probably lived there who could not buy anything from me. At the third house a dog lay on the porch so of course I couldn't approach it. And so, for one reason or another, I walked by a dozen houses. Then I began to realize that if I continued in that manner I wouldn't earn a cent until the Messiah arrived, so I worked up my courage and with a loud beating heart I rang the bell at a nearby house. An angry woman opened the door and before I could say a word she shouted, "Nothing today!" I got away as quickly as possible. So I continued for the rest of the day, stopping at about one out of every five or six houses and it wasn't until late in the afternoon that a woman asked if I had needles. While I was going through my satchel to find the needles she saw some other things she wanted and she bought altogether $3.00 worth of my merchandise. That was my entire business for the first day.

Following Goldshtick's advice, I went to the place he had suggested for a night's lodging. The next morning my bill for supper, lodging and breakfast was $.50 which I paid in merchandise not cash. And because I felt this was very reasonable I also gave the child a gift hoping to gain their good will which might be helpful in the future. When I started out on my peddling the second day I realized that I should stop at every house and make an effort to enter and display my goods, but still my heart had me skipping some houses. In those houses where they wanted to buy but offered less than my price, I refused to sell because I insisted on one price. I wanted them to know that a Jew too was an honest and decent man. In truth I was successful by this manner of doing business because rarely did I sleep in a barn and never did I have to sleep in the open field. Wherever I spent the night I was always invited to be their guest in the future and wherever I made a sale I was always welcomed when I made a second call. I began to build a group of regular customers whom I called on once a month and I knew each day where I would have dinner and where I would spend the night. Wherever I dealt they called me by my first name and they were always happy to see me. In New York in the stores where I bought I acquired a good reputation and good credit. In these areas everything was satisfactory but in the area of making a profit things were not too good.

Such things as justice, conscience and a feeling of honor were not found everyday among big businessmen and certainly not among peddlers. The motto of the peddler was if you want to be somebody, a *mensch,* then you must for a time forget that you are somebody. In practice this meant a peddler should schnorr as much as possible in order to get as much as possible from as many as possible. If you could get 300 percent profit you were to get it; if only 25 percent, that too was acceptable. The main thing was never to lose a customer. The peddler always had to be ready with some kind of an excuse if he were caught in some dishonesty and if he didn't have an explanation he was not to care too much about it. There were enough peasants in America, so went a peddler's phrase — if one of them became angry there was always another one to be found. Most peddlers operated in this manner as did my comrade Schneider. And in so operating they succeeded. But for myself, I could not forget that I was a man, even though I had been a teacher, a farm hand and now a peddler. And so I remained a poor man.

This might sound like self-praise, but believe me this is not my intention because it is not very pleasant to describe myself as a *shlim-mazel,* an unlucky person. If I had not been born and raised to be such a naive person and if I could have followed a more practical system as did most of my fellow peddlers who now occupy important places in the world of business, I would really now be able to praise myself as a great success in business.

I will now tell you something about Schneider with no intention of praising myself or putting him to shame. I will merely recite facts and whether these facts indicate honor or shame is no fault of mine. Schneider was a better peddler than I was. He had the knack of getting into a house even if the people didn't want to let him enter. Furthermore he did not bother with such foolishness as one price and he was a better businessman than I. His main goal was to sell as much as possible. If he could make a profit he would, but he would sell even without profit, his purpose being to increase his volume of sales so he could increase his line of credit. In a remarkably short time he had established sufficient credit to open a store in "White House." There his business increased and his credit increased until...until he emptied his store, closed the shutters and gave his creditors nothing, a fig. Do you think he had any feeling of shame or pang of conscience? God forbid! Instead of feeling ashamed, he was proud of it. Instead of being conscience-stricken, he was happy about it.

One of his creditors was a pants manufacturer, really a poor man. I happened to be in Schneider's store when this manufacturer came in pleading with tear-filled eyes for Schneider to pay his debt and save him from ruin. Schneider listened and said that all he could do was to treat him to a cigar. When the manufacturer began to use harsh words and call Schneider a thief, Schneider threw him out of the now empty store. When I told Schneider I could not do such a thing, he said, "You're nothing but a teacher," by which he meant that he was the smart and clever man and I was the unlucky one. Perhaps he was really correct because I thought that he would lose all his credit, but as a matter of fact when he opened his store again he bought from other people and he obtained greater credit than before, because by now he was worth several thousand dollars. He operated for about another year and then again closed the store, paying nothing to his creditors, having arranged mortgages with a friend. He went to Newark, N.J., bought a fine house and opened a butcher store. I assumed that he opened a non-kosher store because I knew that he was the kind of Jew who had even forgotten where his *tallis* [prayer shawl] and *tefillin* [phylacteries] were and he also had a good appetite for pork and rabbit. It never occurred to me that he could or would operate a kosher butcher store. I felt he would be afraid that someone who knew him would report what kind of *zaddik* [saintly pietist] he was.

Some time later I met him and asked him how he was doing and he said excellent. "Is this a better business than clothing?" I asked "Much better," he answered, "to sell a cheap suit as an expensive one can't be done too easily but to sell a piece of salami made of the poorest quality meat as the best quality was not too difficult as long as one had the know how." "Are your products strictly kosher?" I asked. "Strictly or not strictly," he said, "when the chief rabbi of New York comes to Newark he eats only meat bought at my store and that means that my store is considered the kosher store of Newark." "How can you do this?" I asked. "You're still a teacher," he said.

I never saw him after this encounter but I did hear that he grew quite rich, that he was president of the largest Orthodox synagogue in Newark, and that he was active in politics, even though he could not write the first letter of the Yiddish or English alphabet and associated with the irreligious Jewish socialists. If he had not died an early death he would perhaps have been one of the leaders in the American Jewish community. I must emphasize that telling this story about Schneider I do not intend to single him out, but I use him only as an example to represent many who have become well off and are now leaders in our community.

And now to return to my story. For three years I dragged myself around the country, in heat and in cold, in mud and in snow, a heavy pack on my shoulders, and no great fortune did I acquire. All I was able to accumulate was just enough to maintain my family abroad on a rather poor level of existence. I was not able to accumulate enough to bring them to America until the shipping companies began to compete so strongly that they reduced the passenger fare to eight dollars.

In the early part of 1885 I sent tickets and travel expenses to my family, my wife and seven children, who arrived in Castle Garden in May, 1885, three years after my arrival. But when I arrived I was alone, a stranger with no one to meet me. They, on the other hand, were met by a husband and father with great joy, a father who had made ready a home and made every possible effort to give them a pleasant and comfortable welcome. Along with my family came my mother-in-law and brother-in-law Nissan Bloom. S. S. Bloom (Shmuel) was already in America and not only was he interested in the arrival of his mother and brother, but was most helpful to me and my family. While I was out working in the country collecting as much money as possible, he rented the rooms, obtained the furniture and all that was necessary for my family to start housekeeping.

I must report one other thing he did which shows his friendship and concern. When our bunch arrived they were not a very attractive looking group. They were so green they appeared to be black. Moses, who was 12 years old and considered himself the biggest sport of the whole bunch, was dressed in a long coat made of material used as cheap lining today which at one time had been yellow, and boots with leggings into which his pants had been inserted. Nathan was barefoot because his shoes were so worn out that they had been thrown into the sea. The rest of the group did not look any better. They were surrounded by bundles of various sizes and bedding packed in sheets which had become quite soiled during the trip. Almost as if to be spiteful it was an unusually beautiful spring day and a Sunday when all of New York was dressed up as if for a holiday. Shmuel and I stood there wondering how to transport this group to Orchard Street where we had taken rooms. No express wagon was to be had because it was Sunday. The only thing we could do was to take the elevated train.

Imagine leading a pack of such greenhorns into a car filled with people dressed in their Sunday best, a twelve year old boy dressed for a winter storm on a beautiful spring day, his brother barefoot, his younger sister dressed as for winter, and with kerchiefs on their heads. To Shmuel and to me, who thought of ourselves as completely Americanized, the group seemed so funny and bizarre that we were ashamed to bring them into a car. So after Shmuel and I conferred for a while in English, first because we didn't want the group to know what we were saying and secondly to impress them with our being Americanized, Shmuel said, "Just for today what difference will it make? You take a big bundle, I'll take a bundle, the children will take the smaller bundles. You take half the group in one car and I'll take the other half into another car. As long as they don't throw us off, we'll make out. Tomorrow we'll get them bathed, have their hair cut, buy them clothes and they'll look like American gentlemen and ladies." I followed his suggestion. When my group and I entered the car, the passengers moved away from us and stared but that's all that happened. The next day, not only were they unrecognizable as greenies by others, but they too did not recognize themselves when they looked into a mirror.

I cannot end the description of this period without relating the following joke. When I led my brother-in-law Nissan into the barber shop he was so anxious to show that he was not a complete greenhorn and to show that he knew English that he made a deep bow almost to the floor and said, "Goodbye."

We remained in New York only three or four months. Now that my family was with me my expenses had increased beyond my earnings at that time so I had to move to the country. Our first move was to Princeton, a splendid, quiet town near the Delaware River. This move made a big improvement in our living conditions. Instead of paying $18 per month for four rooms, living like in a chicken coop, we had a comfortable house of eight rooms and a barn for $8 a month and our living expenses were cut more than a half. In addition, both Moses and Nathan, my sons, did some peddling. They didn't bring in any great fortune, but they did bring in a little which helped. Since we had a barn, I bought a horse and wagon which enabled me to carry a greater stock and also made it easier for me than carrying a pack on my shoulders and it also enabled me to get home nearly every night. Furthermore, we were not lonely here in Princeton because my brother-in-law Elias Klein and a certain Abe Cohen, now reverend [sic] in Chester, and a certain Blumenthal, now deceased, lived with us. They all peddled in the area. In addition, other Jewish peddlers would spend a night or a Sunday at our house.

We remained in Princeton only a few months. I rented a larger house, not far from Princeton, having ten large rooms and two barns, a fruit orchard and about eight acres at about the same $8 a month (or to be exact $100 per year) and the house was not far from the station. After we had moved into this new place, I bought a cow and some chickens. I already had a horse, and my desire to be a farmer was again aroused. I felt that this was only a beginning of being a farmer because I would need more land if I was to make my living from farming. But I did not give up peddling entirely. I continued as one half peddler, one quarter farmer and one quarter a new occupation, taking in boarders.

The boarders were not like today's boarders, who pay $1 per night and $2 for dinner. Our boarders were poor peddlers who paid 10¢ for a night's lodging and 15¢ for a meal, and we had more than enough of them. We usually had three every night and on Sundays as many as a dozen. The work involved was more than boarding house operators do today. Today the boarding house operator buys his bread and has beds ready for his boarders. We had to bake our own bread because our boarders and we didn't like to eat non-Jewish bread and every night we had to make up sleeping arrangements for every one. My wife and mother-in-law, who lived with us, were overworked beyond their strength and after all this effort we made only a poor living. After a while my brother-in-law Samuel (Shmuel) Bloom pulled us out of there. Bloom had lived with us when we were in Princeton and he was a peddler at that time. When we moved from Princeton he gave up peddling and went to live in Philadelphia where he worked at his trade, being a jeweler, for $4 per week plus board.

After Bloom had been in Philadelphia a few weeks, he came to visit us and strongly urged us to move to Philadelphia and presented strong facts showing that families like ours were living much better than we were and they were not burdened with the kind of hard labor we were doing. My wife, of course, was in favor of this plan. As for me, I was weighing it in my mind because deep in my heart I still cherished the idea of being a farmer, but in my head I knew that Shmuel and my wife were right. In the end I capitulated and we decided to move to Philadelphia.

---

*Harris Rubin, who was in his mid-eighties
when he died in 1931, had been in his youth a Talmud student
and then a teacher in his native Lithuania.
But what seems to have had the strongest influence upon him
was "the idea of Zionism which held that the future
of Jewish life demanded that Jews become farmers and colonists."
Rubin left a Yiddish autobiography, which was
translated into English by Benson N. Schambelan and privately
published at Philadelphia in the 1970's. The recollections
presented here are an excerpt from that work.*

Alexander Harkavy in 1882

Chapters from My Life

Alexander Harkavy

The years 1881-1882 were trying days for the Jews of Russia owing to the horrors which broke out against them in the southern districts. Many of our brethren in Russia left at that time for America. In Southern Russia, groups of enlightened Jews, products of the new generation, organized to go and settle in America as farmers. In the spring of 1882 such a movement of group organization also began among the enlightened Jewish youth of Vilna. When this news reached me I joined up. According to the regulations of my group every member was obligated to prepare seventy rubles for travel expenses. My relative having no opposition to my desire to travel to America, she agreed to give me the money out of the legacy left by my father, of blessed memory, over which she had control.

Farming was the ideal of intellectual Russian Jews in those days, but as to the means of carrying out this aim they were divided into two factions: one demanded that the immigration be to Palestine to settle the Land of Israel; the other insisted that the immigration be to America. Both sides loved their people dearly; they disagreed only over the site to be chosen. Each group was known by the name of the country which it chose: "Palestinians" and "Americans." The second group was larger than the first. All immigrants who left Russia with the object of taking up farming needed support. The "Palestinians" were helped by rich Jews in Russia; the "Americans" relied upon the Hebrew Emigrant Aid Society, the organization then established in New York to assist refugees.[1]

The group which I joined consisted of twenty intellectual young men, among them former students in the upper grades of the gymnasia who left their studies to devote themselves to working the land. Not one of us knew the nature of this work; we merely were dreamers, alert to every new cry. In Jewish circles the cry then was "work the land." We followed in its wake. We imagined to ourselves that we would easily be able to become farmers, especially on American soil which we presumed a Garden of Eden....

Our group was founded in February 1882. Its first act was to suggest to a larger group — the Am Olam already established in Kiev — to take us in under its flag. We found this desirable because the Kiev group had already exchanged letters with the Hebrew Emigrant Aid Society in New York,[2] and had received its promise to help it achieve its aims once it arrived in America. The Kiev group willingly received our suggestion, and our two groups merged. The name Am Olam devolved also upon us.[3] The two groups then discussed where they would join together, and decided to gather in the port city of Liverpool, England, from where a boat would transport all of us at once to our desired destination. Both groups selected leaders for themselves. The head of the Kiev group was Nicholas Aleinitoff,[4] a university student (who later became a lawyer in New York). Our group's leader was M. Kaspe [Abraham Kaspe][5] a gymnasium student (now a doctor in this city).

Members of our groups used to gather together from time to time to consult with one another on how best to plan our departure. One of the conditions which we agreed upon was to fund our expenses collectively, without giving any advantage to one person or another. Our last gathering was held at the end of April (according to the non-Jewish calendar), outside Vilna on a hill near Zheleznaia Khatka[?]. There we set the day for our departure from Vilna. The day we selected was one of the first days in May. After this meeting, I prepared myself for the journey: I set aside clothes for myself, took leave of friends and relatives scattered around the city, bundled up my belongings which were my books, and began to study the English language.

The day set for our departure from Vilna arrived, and we were ready to go.[6] At ten in the morning every member of our group was supposed to gather by the railway. When the moment came to separate from Vilna, love for my native land welled up within me, and I lamented to myself my decision to set out for America. But everything was set; there was no turning back. Brokenhearted, I parted from my relatives who owned the press and from the auditors in the office of accounting, and I made my way to the railway where members of the group had gathered. Our first destination was a small city in Lithuania near the Prussian border. We arrived there after noon, and turned in at a hotel outside the city. There we found a Jew engaged in border crossing [smuggling]. We contracted with him to cross us into Prussia at a price of three rubles a head. Toward evening the man brought a large wagon which took us as far as the border district. There we got off the wagon, and the man left us alone. He went off to bargain on our behalf with one of the district's residents. No sooner did he leave than we began to fear for our lives. We were terrified that army borderguards would see and catch us. After an hour, our border crosser returned with a Christian man and both quietly ordered us to come along. Trembling mightily we followed them. They led us into Prussia. The border area was filled with wells of water and slime, and we grew impatient at our pace. Finally, after wandering about for half an hour, we came to the city of Eydtkuhnen in Prussia. The short time had seemed to us like an eternity. When told by the men that we were no longer in Russia, our joy knew no bounds.

We arrived in Eydtkuhnen after midnight and made straight for the hotel. There we feasted on bread and ale; we were happy and in high spirits. We were pleased both to have safely succeeded in crossing the border of our cruel native land, and to have placed the soles of our feet down on the soil of Germany — which excelled in higher education and in a legal system designed to benefit its citizens. After having eaten, we lay down to rest from the ardors of our journey. We slept very well indeed. Next morning we woke joyfully, and went out walking to see the city and its inhabitants. We found groups of people and spoke with them about the quality of Germany, and the relationship of its citizens to the government. The residents whom we asked praised both their leaders and their way of life. They told us that Germans were pleased that their government extended human rights to all citizens. I asked one about the relationship of Jews to the army: did some of them try to escape this obligation? The man replied that every one of them enters military service willingly; not only that, they yearn for it even if not admitted. To support his words he told me the story of how in Eydtkuhnen there was a Jew who was not admitted to military service on account of some deformity which was found in him. This man, according to the storyteller, spent a great deal of money in order to be admitted, but he didn't succeed and was terribly disappointed. This

was astonishing to me. I told myself: "see how great the difference is
between Germany and Russia."

We remained in Eydtkuhnen for twenty-four hours, and then travelled on to Hamburg. We remained in this port city for two days. At that
time there was in Hamburg a Jewish committee to support Russian
emigrants who came there by the thousands on their way to America.
We turned to this committee with the request that it purchase for us
tickets on an English boat at the special rate offered charitable
societies. The committee filled our request, and in this way we saved
the treasury of our group some money.

From Hamburg, we travelled over the North Sea to the city of
Hartlepool in England, and from there via train to the port city of
Liverpool. There we were to wait until the Am Olam from Kiev arrived
so that we might go down to the ship along with them. Four days later
the group arrived. Great joy filled our hearts when we learned that our
allied group had made it. In high spirits we rushed to greet them. After
a meeting between the leaders of our two groups, the creation of a legal
union was announced: henceforward, we were like brothers of a single
society. The Kiev group with which we had joined had seventy members, men and women. Most were young intellectual men, dreamers
just like we were. Among its members was the late poet, David
Edelstadt,[7] then about eighteen years old. Our two groups met up with
one another on the afternoon of May 15th. That very day, the ship
British Prince stood at the harbor ready to accept passengers for
America. It was destined to take us as well. Just an hour after our
union we went down to the ship together. That evening the *British
Prince* hoisted anchor, and began to transport us to our ultimate
destination: the new world.

The boat *British Prince* was like a city floating on water, so great
was the number of its passengers. All its passengers were Russian
immigrants; all, save members of our group, were travelling to
America as individuals, seeking to improve their position by their own
brains and brawn; this one through handiwork, that one through
peddling. Members of our group saw themselves as superior to this
multitude. "The other passengers are not like us," said we to ourselves,
"we are not merely going to America for simple comfort, we are
idealists, eager to prove to the world that Jews can work the land!" In
our imagination, we already saw ourselves as landowning farmers

dwelling on our plots in the western part of the country. So certain were we that our aims in the new world would be achieved that even on the boat we began to debate which kind of community institutions we would build, which books we would introduce into our library, whether or not we would build a synagogue and so forth (with regard to the synagogue, most of the views were negative). We danced and sang overcome with joyous expectation of what America held in store for us. In spite of seasickness, storms, and tempests which visited us on our journey, we were happy and lighthearted. All the days of our Atlantic voyage were filled with joy.

On May 30th, fifteen days after our boat set sail from Liverpool, we arrived safely at the North American shoreline and disembarked onto dry land. Our boat stood at the port of Philadelphia in the state of Pennsylvania. Our destination, however, was New York where the Hebrew Emigrant Aid Society was centered, and the next day we were taken there by railroad. Upon our arrival we were brought to a place then known as Castle Garden[8] where we rested from the wearisome journey. Our leader, the head of the Kiev group, went to the administrative office of H.E.A.S. on State Street to inform them of our arrival, and to ask them what they planned to do for us.

Between the time that our group was founded and the time of our arrival large numbers of our brethren had emigrated from Russia and come to New York. So great were their numbers that the shore officers had found it necessary to erect large wooden shacks around Castle Garden to provide them with cover and a place to sleep. The Castle Garden Plaza was filled from one end to the other with immigrants. On the adjoining streets, — State Street, Greenwich Street, and even at the top of Broadway — women sat on the ground, babies in hand, for want of a home. Owing to the flood of Russian immigrants, the aid society was short of means and couldn't undertake great projects on their behalf. All it could do was arrange that the mass of people be provided with bread until such time as the incoming flood would diminish and they could do somewhat more for their benefit.

The officers of the Society received our leader politely, but informed him that in the existing circumstances they could do not a thing for our group. They continued to say, however, that since we had come to America trusting in the Society, they would agree to provide us at the first opportunity with food and lodging. After a short while our leader returned to our camp and told us everything that the Society's officers had said. Our spirits sank. "No more hope of working the land! Our dreams have come to naught! Alas that we have reached such a state!" After a time, however, we calmed down a bit and our spirits improved. When we saw what troubles faced the rest of our brethren wandering about outside, we made peace with our lot and were grateful for the Society's promise to feed us for the time being.

The Hebrew Emigrant Aid Society at that time owned a refugee station in Greenpoint, Long Island, near New York. There they gave immigrants food and lodging for a short time so that they might renew themselves after the ardors of their journey. We were taken to this house on the day we arrived in New York, and stayed there for about a week. We originally thought that we would be maintained there for several weeks, but after just one passed we were informed that the time had come for us to leave. This seemed wrong to us, and we said that we would stay on notwithstanding the demands of the society's lackeys. When the superintendents of the station saw that they could not force us, they set about deceiving us. On the eighth day of our stay, two men came in the name of the New York Society and gently asked us if we would be so kind as to accompany them to the bathhouse to clean ourselves off. Feeling grimy from the boat voyage, we went along gladly. The men brought us on the ferry to New York, and there, right in the middle of the river, told us that there was no more room for us in Greenpoint. As the saying goes, "they had taken us for a ride."

I cannot let pass in silence our own actions at the refugee station. In spite of our idealism we did not act honorably. The reason for this was that the house rules were very strict. The superintendent was a pious old German Jew whose devotion to every rule was absolute. Since we couldn't follow every detail of every rule there were always arguments between us. Many in our group would arouse this man's anger in very strange ways; for example, at night when he was in bed one would begin to yell, another to dance, another to screech like a chicken, another to sing like a cantor, another to sermonize like a preacher, another to spin rhymes like a jester and so forth. When our behavior was brought to the attention of the Society's overseers in New York, they sent several honorable men out to reprove us. But this had no effect at all: the men did as they had earlier, renewing their pranks even more strongly than before.[9]

The superintendents of the immigrant aid society did not abandon us, however. They felt themselves obligated to extend a helping hand until such time as we could depend on ourselves. Once we were brought from Greenpoint to New York, they allocated enough money to support us for a month (which by their estimation was time enough for us to be able to find work), and they rented a large room for us at 4½ Division Street where we could live. They also bought us a stove for cooking, so we could fix ourselves meals. Responsibility for running our house lay with us and we chose among ourselves a cook and food procurer. Cooking was the only work we did in the house. We paid no attention to cleaning which we considered unnecessary. Our furniture consisted of an oven, pots and dishes, a long table, and long wooden benches. We bedded down on the packs which we had carried with us and which were spread over the floor. Since the room was too narrow to accommodate us all, the women and one or two of the men took beds for the night in one of the nearby hotels.

So long as we lived in our group lodging, we paid no attention to the fact that in a short time we would have to go out on our own. We didn't worry ourselves about tomorrow; we spent our time at home. Between meals somebody would pace up and down the width of the room with a book on the syntax of the Russian language reading in great rapture examples of that language's classical poetry. Some other member was pacing the breadth of the room with a volume by the Polish poet Adam Mickiewicz[10] which he read moving his lips lustily. Another sat quietly in a corner writing a poem or an article. Near the stove stood a group of boys fighting with the cook over the small portions he gave them at mealtime. On the floor, on top of our scattered bundles, several people were lying on their backs, hands folded, looking upward and yawning. The same scenes could be seen in our Division Street room almost every day.

One day, while we were living in this apartment, a fine looking guest appeared before us: Abraham Cahan of Vilna who had arrived in America about six weeks[11] after we had. He would come by our home to spend his time, being as miserable as we members of Am Olam were. Who could have predicted that this man would have risen to the station which he commands today? It is worth mentioning here that one of the members of our group was the widow, Mrs. Anna Bronstein from Kiev who later [December 11, 1886] became his wife.

Several of the men among us became exceptions to the rule: they decided to seek their livelihood by their own sweat and blood, and set out in search of some sort of job. Two or three became independent peddlers, and several others, myself among them, decided to seek salaried employment. In those days it was easy to find work unloading ships, since the stevedores had called a strike. We at that time did not understand the meaning of "strikes" and "scabs," and sought jobs on the ships without knowing whether we would succeed in finding any or not. The supervisors of the loading dock accepted us willingly and put us to work. Our job consisted of wheeling wheelbarrows to the bridges of the ship, loading them up with boxes or sacks full of merchandise, and transporting them to the warehouse next to the harbor. It was very difficult work, and on our first day we returned home totally exhausted, not an ounce of strength left in us. By the second day we had grown accustomed to our work and we didn't strain so hard at it.

The boxes and sacks that we unloaded from the boat were filled with produce from various kinds of trees: almonds, nuts, figs, dates, raisins and others. While working with this merchandise we were overcome with the desire to enjoy some of it. Unable to contain ourselves, we treated the merchandise as one does his own goods: we opened sacks and crates and ate as much as we liked without being disturbed, as there was nobody watching over us. We earned $1.70 a day, but the number of days we spent at the work was few. The original workers, striking for higher wages interfered. After our first week of work, on the day we were to get paid, we were told to be prepared for a settlement of the strike. When we left the supervisors' office there stood in our path groups of strikers laying in wait for "the scabs." They fell upon us. Loading dock supervisors were forced to call out the police to accompany us on our way. After that, we did not go back to work.[12]

When our month of living on Division Street came to an end, our group split up and members went their independent ways. Prior to our separation, each of us received from our leader, a portion of the remaining general fund which he controlled. Everyone's part was equal — five dollars — and that small sum was supposed to provide for us on our new path in life. Then members split up, going off in all directions in search for food. Each man proceeded according to his own wisdom and inclinations.

I set my sights toward work in the fields. Landowners were at that time seeking hands from among the European immigrant peoples. During the week after our group separated, I went to the employment office for refugees then maintained at Castle Garden, and on that very day they found me an employer: an estateholder in the village of Pawling in Dutchess County, New York. The estateholder designated my salary as twelve dollars a month, plus food, and on that very day — July 6th, six weeks after my arrival — he brought me to his estate.

An amusing incident befell me between my departure from New York and my arrival in Pawling. Since the estateholder was Christian, I had decided not to eat meat, lest I be defiled by pig-meat. I had always been careful about this, not from devotion to the laws of permitted and forbidden food but simply from revulsion to pork. While at the railroad station, my employer took me to the cafeteria to eat with him. At the table, the waiter brought both of us a cut of meat looking to me like pork. I didn't eat it. Seeing that I didn't eat the meat, my employer took the menu and allowed me to choose whatever I wanted. I pointed out to the waiter a line which, as I understood it, designated some kind of food made with eggs. The item had two words in it, the first being egg. But I didn't know what the second word meant, my knowledge of English being very slight. The waiter filled my order and, much to my astonishment brought me an expensive drink made from eggs. My employer realized my error and couldn't restrain his laughter.

We reached Pawling in the evening. In my employer's house the table was already set for dinner, to which the mistress of the house immediately summoned me. The table was filled with various foods including several sorts of meat, all of which looked to me like hateful pork products. I ate no meat, and when asked about it by my employer, I falsely told him that the only meat eaten by Russians is chicken! I said this because I couldn't well distinguish pork from other kinds of meat, and I feared that I might someday guess wrong and fall into eating that which I so despised. My employer was amazed that Russians were so finicky, and found the foreign ways very funny. Instead of meat, he ordered that I be given fried fish.

I was given no work to do on the day of my arrival. After dinner, the mistress of the house assigned me a bedroom and I lay down to rest at once so that I would have the strength to work the next morning. At four o'clock the next morning, my employer awakened me and took me with him to teach me my work.

The first thing they taught me on the estate was how to milk a cow. I learned this in one lesson and was henceforward responsible for milking eight cows every morning and evening. During the first couple of days, I found this work very difficult. The cows grazing in the meadows used to run away from me, and I had to chase after each one in order to catch it. While chasing one, another sometimes came and kicked over the bucket of milk I had just taken from the previous cow.

During the rest of the day, I worked in the fields or in the meadows: ploughing land, trampling down dry grass in the carts, and cutting with a scythe hay that couldn't be cut by machine. (Hay was harvested by machine in this region, but in hilly areas it had to be cut by hand.) I used to work not less than sixteen hours a day.

My daily schedule on the farm was as follows. From four to seven in the morning I milked the cows. At seven I ate breakfast, and then immediately went out to work in the fields until lunch at noon. After lunch I went back to the fields until it was time to milk the cows a second time at six. That labor accomplished, I ate dinner, generally at eight. At nine I went to sleep. Sunday was my day of rest, but I couldn't relax entirely: I still had to feed the housepets, help my employer harness up his horses and sharpen his pruning hooks and axes, and perform other small housechores. When during the day I had time for rest and relaxation, I used to study English from a youth, the grandson of the estateholder, or I used to read [Rabbi Joseph Albo's] *Sefer Ha'ikarim*,[13] the only book I brought with me from New York.

During my first two weeks, I felt myself newly invigorated and was happy. The beautiful vision of farm life excited me and made my work a joy. As time went on, however, my strength ebbed, and the work became loathsome to me. I decided to return to New York, but to wait until the month ended so I could get my full month's salary....

On the same plot, there was another Jewish youth working, a Russian immigrant whom my employer brought from New York a couple of days before or after me—I don't remember which. This youth didn't like the work from the beginning, but he too waited out his month.

Immigration bureau scene, New York, circa 1910
(William Williams Collection, New York Public Library)

On the morning of August 16th, a month after I arrived in Pawling, we — my friend and I — informed the estateholder of our decision to leave and demanded our wages — twelve dollars a person according to the contract made with us. Our words shocked him. It was a period when the work in the fields was great, and our labor was very much needed. He entreated us to stay with him, but our resolve being firm as a rock, we refused. Seeing that his request would remain unfulfilled, he decided to deprive us of some of our wages saying "just as you abandon me at a time when work is most necessary, causing me to lose time and money in finding others to replace you, so I shall give you only a portion of your salaries." But even this made no difference. We were stubborn, preferring to lose part of our salary than to remain on the estate. After some bitter words, our employer gave each of us four or six dollars and we left him.

We set out from the farm to the railway station to buy tickets for the journey to New York. On the way, however, we realized how little money we had: "if we spend it all on the railway trip we'll come to our destination almost empty handed." After discussing our situation for a while, we decided to travel to New York on foot. And so we did.

The distance from Pawling to New York is about eighty miles. The railroad traverses this distance in two to three hours; it took us two and half days. We could have made the journey in less time, but we didn't rush. There was no need to; nothing was waiting for us in New York. When we passed a lake or a pond, we would stop and bathe our bodies in the water. When we came to a village or a town we lingered to see the place and the people. In addition, we sometimes were delayed watching out for trains on our path (we walked along the railroad track), especially when we crossed narrow railway bridges. At night we went to the side of the track, in a place of grass or trees, and rested using our packs as pillows, until the morning light. These nights were torture. We were dressed in light summer clothes which were soaked by the cold dew. On one of the two nights, we turned into the thicket where in addition to the plague of dew we were hit with the second plague of the [Passover] *hagadah:* lying on the earth exhausted from several hours of nonstop walking, we were jumped upon by frogs!...

On our way from Pawling to New York, we came upon a company of men laying water pipes. As we passed, their supervisor approached us and offered us work at the rate of $1.50 a day. We turned him down.

On August 18th, in the afternoon, we arrived at the outskirts of New York. There we got on the subway and came down into the city until Bowery Street. I lingered there a while, and then turned toward the immigrant house at Castle Garden.

When I came to Castle Garden, I found a vast throng of people there, one larger than before my trip from New York to the estate. My month away from the city seemed to me like a long time, and I had hoped to find the number of our brethren at Castle Garden dwindling. But I was most mistaken. The square was even more full of people than it had been a month before, for on top of the old immigrants there now were new ones. I found many of my friends from Vilna and Kiev straying aimlessly among this throng. They were amazed that I left the estate at a time when so many of our brethren were circling the streets of New York wrapped in hunger, and they reproved me for my recklessness. The reproof was like a sword piercing my soul. My heart filled with remorse at having left the place where my needs were abundantly provided for.

"What do I do now?" was the question facing me. My friends advised me to return to my employer in Pawling. But that I didn't have the courage to do. After a good deal of soul searching, it occurred to me to go and seek work on the water pipes that I had passed on my way from Pawling to New York. I made the same suggestion to my friends, and three of them accepted it. Three days after returning to New York, my three friends and I set out on foot for the road leading up to the pipes.

The water system on which we sought to work was near the city of White Plains, New York. We left in the morning and walked all day long. At night we rested by the railway station near our destination. Beside the track stood empty cars and with the permission of the stationmasters, who took pity on us, we lay down for the night in one of them. Word of the Jewish immigration from Russia to America had become universally known; the unfortunate refugees roused the compassion of everyone in this country.

The next morning we moved forward on our way and reached the area of the pipes. We found the supervisory men and told them what we wanted. They received us cheerfully, but to our utter disappointment told us they hadn't need of any new workers.

Broken in spirit we returned to New York and became part of the vast throng at Castle Garden. The plight of immigrants then was horribly bitter. Like sucklings at their mother's breast, the immigrants were entirely dependent on help from the Hebrew Emigrant Aid Society. It couldn't help them much; the best it could do was provide a portion of food to prevent their starving to death. For this purpose, the society set up free kitchens on Greenwich Street where people came in groups, one after another. The meals they received, at the Society's expense were poor and skimpy. The operators of the kitchens were eager to make money, and oppressed the unfortunate diners. At breakfast, for which the Society paid ten cents a head, they provided a cup of coffee looking like muddy water, and a loaf of bread worth less than a penny. Whenever mealtime came there was tumult and excitement, since everyone was hungry and eager to be among the first. Those who came to eat had to bring certification tickets from the Society. One of its officers distributed them, signed by him, to the throngs outside. This distribution demanded a great deal of time, and everyone waited his turn impatiently. Many used to forge tickets to fill their empty bellies quicker.

At times, the unfortunate immigrants on Castle Garden wearied of bearing their bitter fate. Stirred by inner passion they would begin to riot. Honorable gentlemen from the Society used then to come, appeal to them, and quiet them down.

The scenes that took place among the despairing immigrants broke the hearts of all onlookers. One, which I shall describe, affected the entire square. A young man, enveloped in hunger, who had not worn a clean shirt for many days, burst into the offices of the directors of the Society on State Street, tore off his contaminated shirt, and cried out loudly "See what has become of me!" Professor Michael Heilprin,[14] of blessed memory, was then sitting in the directors' offices. At the sight of this horrible spectacle he burst into tears and wept like a baby.

Immigrants faced these troubles because they knew so little about the practical world. The year 1882 was a prosperous one in the United States, and work was available for thousands of people. But our brother immigrants didn't understand how ripe the times were. Several among them became wise to it and did improve their positions, but only a few. Intellectuals suffered particularly acutely, for they had come to work the land, which proved impossible. Their hopes dashed, they thought that theirs was no way to live — and therefore did nothing at all. But the practical spirit pervading this country eventually made an impact upon them. Toward the end of the summer, they began to rouse from their slumber.

As summer waned, the throng at Castle Garden began to decrease. Immigrants slowly spread out over the city seeking work or setting up in business. My friends and I also set out to find means of support. Our first concern was to find somewhere to live. Several among us succeeded in locating residences where advance payment was not required; the rest of us were left with nothing. I was among the unfortunates who couldn't find a place to live. For several nights I slept on the floor of a house on Ludlow Street in which some of my friends resided. I considered it my right to dwell in the vestibule of a house where my brethren were living. How I fed myself, I no longer even recall.

During this period of trouble, I sought work through the want ad section of the German language paper that was published in this city: *The New York Staats-Zeitung.* One day I found an ad in this journal seeking a dishwasher for a cafeteria. It being still morning, I raced to the appointed place as soon as I read the ad, and to my great joy was accepted. I assumed that my work would only be to clean bowls, spoons, and knives, but after I was accepted the owner gave me a large pot to clean, encrusted on its bottom and sides with a dry layer of day-old cooking. The owner instructed me to take the pot outside and set it up near the waterpump so that I might have enough water to rinse it. I started to do my work most eagerly, but the crust of food in the pot was very hard and I couldn't remove it. I realized at once that there was no use in my staying on in the cafeteria and I decided to leave. But I was too embarrassed to tell my boss, and sought a way to get out without his knowing. I looked about here and there, found an opening in the corner of the yard, and quickly escaped through it. I felt sorry for the honest owner who on account of me undoubtedly was late serving his guests lunch on that day.

At this time, I became acquainted with a young man from Vilna who worked in a factory which made copper utensils. He advised me to apply for work in his place. Though I knew nothing about the art of coppersmithing, I nevertheless took his advice and applied to the boss for some sort of employment. The overseer accepted me readily, and immediately put me to work. First they taught me how to use a file. Several days later they taught me how to finish copper instruments on a lathe. I became skilled in all facets of the work. My salary at the factory began at two dollars a week and after several weeks it was raised to four. The work lasted ten hours a day: from seven in the morning until six at night (with an hour off for lunch). I spent my spare time studying English and writing articles. One of the pieces which I wrote was the story of Johann Gutenberg, inventor of the printing press.

I considered myself a successful man. But lo, my success didn't last long. After three months, work at the factory declined and I was fired.

After being fired from the factory, I found work as a dishwasher in a restaurant then owned by an immigrant downtown at the corner of Ludlow and Canal streets. The work was hard, and my salary was very low. After two weeks I left the place to find better and more respectable work.

I left the restaurant with just one dollar in my pocket. That was all the money which my boss gave me for two weeks of work. Half of this sum I spent on a week's rent; the rest I set aside to subsist on until I could find a job. I had hoped that I would succeed in finding the means to earn a living in just a few days, but my hopes went unrealized, and I was in trouble. After five days, I had emptied my pocket of its last penny; after a week, I was left without a place to sleep. The man with whom I boarded refused to keep me in his house unless I paid him for a week in advance. I was left without shelter.

So as not to die of starvation or freeze from the cold — which had by then already arrived — I returned to the portals of my poor friends who had succeeded better than I. I joined in their paltry meals and meager accommodations. But even in this I faced obstacles: the owners of those dwellings where my good friends resided refused to permit unregistered guests to stay there, particularly not after dark. On account of these evil men I once had to spend a whole night under the stars.

I'll never forget that night. The cold was fierce and my clothes were torn and tattered. Afraid to sleep in the hall of a house, or in one of the carts that stood outside, I was forced to spend the whole night circling the streets. I strayed hither and yon, going past Bowery and Canal Streets many times. Whenever I reached the elevated subway stop on Canal and Allen I would look at the clock on top of the station to see how many hours were left until sunrise. Time passed exceedingly slowly. When I discovered, after a long hike, that the clock's hour hand had passed five, my spirits brightened. I still couldn't go to anyone's house, but at least I could take joy in the hope that the light of day would soon dawn, and then I could knock at somebody's door. . . .

In the end I succeeded in finding quarters at the home of some good-hearted people who agreed to take me in on condition that I pay them their rent when I earned it.

Meanwhile, it came time to begin baking Passover matzah in the Jewish area of New York. Seeing that I couldn't find a job in a factory, I decided to apply for work in a matzah bakery. This came easily: the first bakery I applied to accepted me at once. Matzah bakeries in those days paid their workers a very low wage, and people used to leave after just a few days on the job — so it was very simple to find work there. All the workers in the matzah bakery were newly arrived immigrants who could easily be cheated and sucked dry by the bakers. In accepting someone for work, they didn't tell him his salary in advance, but allowed him to labor a whole week to see how much his work was worth. After a week was over, they fired the poor "greener" with a pittance. The hours of work in the bakery were from two in the morning until nine or ten at night.

My job at the bakery was to turn the wheel of the machine that kneaded and pressed the dough. It was very hard work, and exceeded my power which had been weakened by hunger and tension. Still I gathered the last of my strength and performed the work satisfactorily. Lacking the money to buy food, I fed myself on the bakery's matzahs which workers were permitted to eat to their heart's content. But I grew to loathe this "bread of affliction" and I awaited the week's end with anticipation to discover what wages my toil would bring. I expected that my pay would be not less than five dollars, but when payday came I discovered that I was greatly mistaken. The amount which the baker gave me for my week of work was $2.50. Seeing this, I became embittered and left this terrible job.

This time, only a few days passed before I found work. One of my friends then worked in a factory where they made cakes of soap and they needed a man for the work. My friend informed me of this, I applied to the factory, and they accepted me. My job was to pound a kind of pitch, melt it into a pot, and dip into it the cakes of soap (they used to dip them in pitch to protect them from the air). My pay at this work was five dollars a week, and I was very pleased with my lot. But lo, after several weeks I had to leave because the dust and smell of the pitch greatly damaged my health. The work was so bad that I fell ill.

When my health returned, I decided not to go back to any sort of "dirty" work, but instead to seek my livelihood in a job that was clean and pleasing to me. It was not long before this work found me of itself.

On East Broadway in New York there was, in those days, an old book-seller named Jerucham S. Kantrowitz. Thanks to his business ties with the firm of "The Widow and the Brothers Romm"[15] in Vilna, I became connected with him, and I made his business my address for letters. On this account I used frequently to visit him, and in this way he learned about me and became interested in my plight. Once when I came to him, he offered me a job as his assistant in the business. I accepted willingly, for not only did I consider the job to be physically easy, but I found it pleasant to be surrounded by books. My salary was exceedingly low — not more than two dollars a week — but my boss often invited me to dine with him and I became like a member of his household. Here I renewed my strength and forgot my poverty. The work was light and easy; I had time to fulfill my old lust for spiritual matters. In my spare time I learned the language of the country, and I increased my knowledge of those subjects which I had studied in the old world.

Kantrowitz's business was in an excellent spot in New York. In those days there were in this city only three [Jewish] booksellers,[16] and Mr. Kantrowitz was the largest of them. He not only stocked prayer-books and books needed by the Orthodox, but also English and German language prayerbooks, scholarly works, and sermons in German by German rabbis like Jellinek[17] used by American Reform rabbis. Thanks to this, his business became a meeting place for great minds. Among those who visited his house were Russian intellectuals, famous German Reform rabbis, and Orthodox rabbis and preachers from Russia and Poland who interested me greatly. One of his visitors was the lawyer J. P. Solomon, founder of the English weekly the *Hebrew Standard.*[18]

While I was comfortable in the bookstore, I did not find any real purpose to my work. I spent my time thinking out how I might attain the life that I had aspired to from my youth. I concluded that the first step in that direction should be teaching. So after two years, I left the bookstore and became a private language teacher. Teaching in those days did not command a large salary from among our European immigrant brethren. But the hope that it would lead me to my goal of becoming a writer was compensation enough.

I cannot close this chapter without describing my boss, the bookseller, who was one of New York's exceptional people in the eighties of the last century. Mr. Kantrowitz was an excellent character in every way. Though old and Orthodox, when I knew him, he always wore a top hat and the latest fashion clothes. Every day, after morning prayers and before breakfast, he used to learn a chapter of Mishnah or Gemara with a group of Jews from his homeland in the small synagogue above his business. Among our brethren in New York City and State he was very important — a giant to whom all would turn in matters of Jewish concern. He was a treasurer of the Rabbi Meir Ba'al Hanes charity [for the poor of Eretz Israel], and a *mohel* [ritual circumciser] who took no money for his efforts, save asking affluent coreligionists to donate to his charity. But this was not the only reason why he was loved; he was also clever and witty.... Once, before Rosh Hashanah a small congregation in New York State asked him to send them a young cantor for the holy days. He knew an old cantor, over seventy, and sent him to the place just a day before the holidays, so that the congregation wouldn't have time to return him. Immediately after Rosh Hashanah he received a letter from the congregation reproving him for his action. He replied, "I know that the cantor I sent you had just been married. I didn't ask how old he was." (The cantor had just entered the bonds of matrimony for the third time!)

I said above that there were three booksellers in New York. The second largest was Hyman Sakolski who deserves to be mentioned here. His business was limited to prayerbooks (*sidurim* and *machzorim*) in English and German editions that he printed from plates bought from the printer, [Henry] Frank, the founder of a Hebrew press in New York in the forties of the nineteenth century.[19] Sakolski came to America in the sixties of that century and it is said that he began his activities in a unique way. Knowing that there were many cities in the state where small Jewish settlements existed far removed from Jewish life, unable to found communities or synagogues, he made a business of bringing to places like this a wagon with a Torah, a *talit* [prayer shawl] and *tefilin* [phylacteries]. Wherever he went, he suggested to isolated Jews that they put on the *talit* and *tefilin* while he read to them a portion from the Torah (even on days of the week when no Torah portion is read). Jews received him eagerly and paid him well. In this way he accumulated capital and established his bookdealership. He was a handsome, well-dressed man, and in his day was one of the most honored Jews in New York.

The period which I am recounting was an ideal one for Jews immigrating to America!

Alexander Harkavy (1863-1939) is today best known
for his pioneering Yiddish-English-Hebrew Dictionary *(1925, rev. 1928),*
but early East European immigrants knew him for his
immigrant-aid books: volumes which taught Yiddish-speaking
newcomers to speak and read in English, to correspond
in English, and to better understand their newly adopted land.
Harkavy taught, lectured, edited several newspapers, and wrote —
voluminously — in five languages (Yiddish, Hebrew,
Russian, German, English). In his Hebrew autobiography (1935),
Prakim Mechayai (Chapters from My Life), most of which was first
published in the Hebrew journal Haleum *(1903), he described his*
childhood in Byelorussia, his four years in Vilna, and his first trying
days on American soil.[20] *The excerpts appearing*
here were translated and annotated by Dr. Jonathan D. Sarna, of
the Hebrew Union College faculty in Cincinnati.

Notes

1. See Joel S. Geffen, "Whither: To Palestine or to America in the Pages of the Russian Hebrew Press, *Ha-Melitz* and *Ha-Yom* (1880-1890)," *American Jewish Historical Quarterly,* 59 (1969), pp. 179-200.

2. See Gilbert Osofsky, "The Hebrew Emigrant Aid Society of the United States (1881-1883)," *Publications of the American Jewish Historical Society (=PAJHS),* 49 (1960), pp. 173-85.

3. Abraham Menes, "The Am Oylom Movement," *Yivo Annual of Jewish Social Studies,* IV (1949), pp. 9-33.

4. The memoirs of Nicholas Aleinikoff (1861-1921) dating to this period may be found in H. Burgin, *Geshichte fun der Idisher Arbeiter Bavegung in Amerika* (New York, 1915), pp. 76-77, partly translated in Melech Epstein, *Jewish Labor in U.S.A.* (rev. ed. New York, 1969), I, pp. 22-23.

5. On Abraham Kaspe (1860-1920) see *Universal Jewish Encyclopedia,* VI (1942), p. 331.

6. For what follows, compare the memoirs of Harkavy's fellow passenger Gregory Weinstein in his *The Ardent Eighties and After* (New York, 1947) esp. pp. 6-10 Burgin. *Idisher Arbeiter Bavegung,* pp. 74-75, lists other notable members of this Am Olam unit.

7. David Edelstadt (1866-1892) was an early Jewish socialist poet. His untimely death, of tuberculosis, transformed him into a folk hero of the labor movement. *Encyclopaedia Judaica,* VI (1972), cols. 364-65.

8. Philip Taylor, *The Distant Magnet* (New York, 1971), pp. 126-7; George J. Svejda, *Castle Garden as an Immigrant Depot, 1855-1890* (Washington: National Parks Service, 1968).

9. Compare Leo Shpall (ed.), "The Memoir of Doctor George Price," *PAJHS,* 47 (1957), pp. 102-106.

10. Adam Mickiewicz (1798-1855) was a Polish nationalist poet who expressed sympathy for Jews (his mother was descended from a converted Frankist family), and had some influence on Hebrew literature. *Encyclopaedia Judaica,* XI, cols. 1500-1501; A. Duker in Waclaw Lednicki, *Adam Mickiewicz in World Literature* (Berkeley, 1956), pp. 561-68.

11. Cahan actually arrived on June 6th, only seven days after Harkavy. See Abraham Cahan, *The Education of Abraham Cahan,* translated by Leon Stein, Abraham P. Conan, and Lynn Davison (Philadelphia, 1969), pp. 217, 222; and Moses Rischin in *Dictionary of American Biography,* supplement V (1977), pp. 95-97.

12. For other, somewhat different accounts of this pivotal incident, see Weinstein, *Ardent Eighties,* p. 15; George Price, "The Russian Jews in America," translated by Leo Shpall, *PAJHS* 48 (1958), p. 40; Cahan, *Education,* p. 234; I. Kopeloff, *Amol in Amerika* (Warsaw, 1928), pp. 53-56; and Irving Howe, *World of Our Fathers* (New York, 1976), pp. 102-103.

13. *Sefer Ha-Ikarim* (1425), *The Book of Principles,* is a famous treatise on Jewish articles of faith composed to counter declining Jewish morale and increased wavering of belief. See Alexander Altmann in *Encyclopaedia Judaica,* II, cols. 535-37.

14. Michael Heilprin (1828-1888) was born in Poland and immigrated to America in 1856. He attained fame as a writer and encyclopedist. Toward the end of his life he became active in Jewish relief work, winning unstinting praise even from otherwise hostile immigrants. See *Dictionary of American Biography,* 8 (1932), p. 502; and Gustav Pollak, *Michael Heilprin and His Sons* (New York, 1912).

15. The Romm Press (1789-1940) in Vilna was the most prestigious and probably the wealthiest Jewish press in Europe toward the end of the nineteenth century. Harkavy had served in its bookkeeping department before immigrating to America.

16. For a list of New York bookstores in 1890, see J.D. Eisenstein *Autobiography and Memoirs* (New York, 1929), p. 66 (in Hebrew).

17. Adolf Jellinek (1820/21-1893) was a Viennese rabbi and scholar who ranked among the greatest preachers of his day. See Moses Rosenmann, *Dr. Adolf Jellinek, sein Leben and Schaffen* (Vienna, 1931).

18. Jacob P. Solomon (1838-1909) was an immigrant from England, a noted lawyer, and the editor of the Orthodox weekly, the New York *Hebrew Standard* (1881-1920). *American Jewish Year Book,* 6 (1904-5), p. 190; Eisenstein, *Autobiography,* p. 117.

19. Henry Frank (1804-1868) immigrated to America from Germany in 1848, and at his death was New York's foremost Hebrew printer and publisher. Madeleine B. Stern, "Henry Frank: Pioneer American Hebrew Publisher," *American Jewish Archives,* 20 (November 1968), pp. 163-168.

20. (Jacob Shatzky), *Harkavy's Bio-Bibliography* (New York, 1933); A.R. Malachi, *Mascot Ur'shumot* (New York, 1937), pp. 173-77 (in Hebrew); Bernard G. Richards, "Alexander Harkavy," *American Jewish Year Book* 42 (1940), pp. 153-64; Yudel Mark, "Alexander Harkavy," *Jewish Book annual* 26 (1966), pp. 100-108 (in Yiddish).

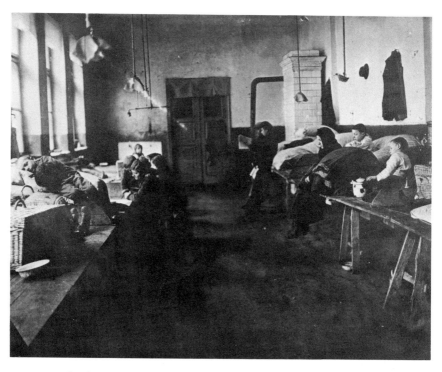

On the way to America: a dormitory for Jewish emigrants in Warsaw

Letters of an Immigrant

Isaac Don Levine

July 5, 1914

This is written on the day of my arrival to Kanasas City, forty-eight hours after I landed at Boston. Together with six other immigrants we were placed on a train going west, and in less than two days made the distance of about two thousand *versts,* changing trains only once — at Chicago. At home the same distance between Vilna [Vilnius] and Orenburg is made in six days, changing trains on the way not less than eight times.

On the train the most striking thing to me was the perfect order of the passengers and the quietness reigning everywhere. You hear no noisy conversations, no annoying laughter. Big trunks are not allowed into the passenger cars, and the handbags or suitcases are conveniently placed on specially attached shelves. There is a separate compartment or, sometimes, a special car for smokers.

We were the objects of continuous curiosity, and the farther west we went the more attention we attracted. But in no way were we insulted by anybody. One old man even attempted to converse with me, but as he knows no other language except English I could not make him out. The conductor was very kind and attentive to us all the time; he often shook his head and said, "All right, all right!"

All-right is the only word I understand of the language of Shakespeare and Byron. I heard it spoken hundreds of times by the immigration and customs inspectors, conductors, porters, truck men and passengers. Its sense must be very broad, for it is used on thousands of different occasions by everybody.

Hyman met me at the station. Smoothly shaved, in a snow-white collar, with the diamond rings on his fingers and the heavy-golden chain of his watch attached to the vest, he looked like a Rothschild. But a minute later I noticed a group of similar Rothschilds waiting for the other immigrants.

I had a postal card to mail home and Hyman showed me a letter-box. I had some difficulty in understanding the mechanism of the box, and for two or three minutes Hyman had a healthy laugh. In justice to the American postal system I must say that the letter-boxes are smaller, safer and simpler than ours. The mail is taken out very frequently, and a case of a letter being delivered after twenty-five years traveling, as it has happened in Kiev, is hardly possible in this land of business.

When Hyman went to inquire about my baggage I found myself surrounded by several prying boys who examined me from every side and very closely. One of them gazed at me for quite a while and I began to feel very uncomfortable, when a policeman appeared on the scene and the little inquisitors disappeared.

The policeman resembled more Goliath than David. Before being given a position of a policeman, one must pass a very rigid examination and must be of certain weight and height. My rescuer was a fine specimen of manhood neatly dressed and of a dignified bearing. He had no saber on his side, instead he held a club in his hand and frightened me not a little by swinging it back and forth.

I had another interesting experience in the baggage room. I lost my blue slip — the receipt — and could not get my things. Hyman tried to persuade me to go home with him and to return the following day and see what can be done about it. I protested and declared that I would not leave the station without my property. After long talks with several officials, he succeeded in getting it. It will be delivered here in the house by a company.

This is the land of companies and trusts. Downstairs in the basement, a poor shoemaker keeps his shop over which hangs the following sign "Brockton Shoe Repairing Company." I wondered what a company it is, and asked Hyman about it. He said the shoemaker scarcely makes eight-nine dollars a week, but that such is the "American style."

The conductors on the street car don't accept any foreign money. When I wanted to pay our fare with a ten kopeck coin Hyman pulled me by the sleeve, winked to the conductor, paid him, but received no tickets. When the conductor receives a passenger's fare, he pulls a cord and rings it off a clock-like self-registering machine. They don't steal, first, because the people are honest in this country, and, second, the railway employs private detectives to watch them.

I noticed on the street car two rows of leather straps hanging on both sides of the car for the convenience of the standing public. I cannot understand why they should not have at home the same useful device. The car is somewhat larger than ours and its speed is much greater, although, at times, it moved very slowly, for the streets were crowded and the automobiles seem to be countless.

The house and the street where Hyman lives amazed me. The pavement is in a very poor condition and the noise of the playing children, street cars and wagons is awful. You meet colored people everywhere, and they seem to be more numerous than the whites. Most of them are very poor and ignorant.

Hyman's wife is a good housekeeper and is very well Americanized. I scarcely understand her, because her speech is full of English phrases and she tries to emphasize them strongly. Several "landswomen" [women from Levine's district in Byelorussia] were expecting me and for an hour they poured on me a rain of questions about home news. Their husbands were at work, and I understand that Hyman wasted half a day's work on account of me.

The dinner appealed to my appetite, and I think a lot of the American dishes. For the first time in my life I ate today a banana, a fruit very cheap in this country. There are many other fruits which at home can be bought in the big cities only for expensive prices, while here they are very common.

Towards evening we went out into the main part of the city. The flood of electric light almost blinded my eyes. The crowds on the sidewalks were very thick. Some of the buildings are very tall, and one of them is a real skyscraper. I counted sixteen stories and almost felt a headache. Hyman says there is one of fifty-five stories in New York. My imagination refuses to work over it. At home such things are counted among the many unexisting miracles said to be found in America. But this is a reality, and how they are constructed is absolutely incomprehensible to my mind.

We passed a schoolhouse, and I found it rather large, surrounded by a spacious, clean yard, but ugly looking. It is a red brick building and it reminds me of a jail at home or of a soldiers' quarterhouse. The American flag was waving over it and my aesthetic feelings were fully satisfied looking at it. I think it is the most beautiful banner in the world.

We returned home loaded with packages. I find the prices of clothes pretty low here, and Hyman said that in the East everything is much cheaper than here. After a short visit to a nearby barber shop, where the barber proved to be an immigrant from my own country, I enjoyed a bath. Every house, except very old ones, is equipped with a bath, and there are so many improvements that, after all, the rent is not as high as it sounds as first.

In an hour I was transformed into an "American," and even Hyman's wife said that I don't look "green" at all. I had a hard struggle with the collar, and after a fifteen-minute fruitless effort to put it on right I commenced to curse the twentieth-century civilization. The American clothes lack grace and elegance, but provide comfort, and the shoes are really not [to] be excelled and deserve the universal credit given to them.

The usual notion at home that only electric light is used in America is not true. Electric light is too expensive and the poorer class of people light their house by gas, which is furnished by a company. Hyman's wife gave me a long lecture about the properties of the gas and how to light it or put out the light. Many suicides in this country are committed through this gas and, [despite] the intention of going to bed now, [I was] greatly worried over this dangerous [ether] flowing in a pipe not far from [my] bed.

July 12, 1914

In the American schools most of the teachers are ladies, and some of these ladies are old maids with kind hearts, but not pretty looks. My good fortune, however, followed me even to the night school and I happened to fall into the room of a very pretty young girl. She teaches with all heart and soul, and seemingly enjoys the work immensely. But sometimes she makes her self very ridiculous and causes an indescribable uproar of laughter from the class which speaks a dozen of different languages. The other evening she had to explain the difference between "to skip" and "to jump," and being, of course, dressed in the latest hobble fashion she illustrated the meaning of those words by actually performing what their meaning implies, which reminded me of a grasshopper.

I am the best pupil in the class and the teacher thinks a lot of me, but it came to pass a short time ago that while reading aloud I struck the word "to wait" and I did not know its meaning. The pretty Miss Stone tried to explain it to me and talked for about fifteen minutes. She made all kinds of movements with her hands, she pointed to the clock on the wall and, although I was sorry to disappoint her, my intelligence still refused to comprehend it, and moreover, it confused in my mind several other words. Luckily a gentleman friend of the teacher entered the room. He knew German and promptly came to help by pronouncing *warten* in that language. It seemed so simple to me then that I was wondering how I did not grasp it before.

There is one great trouble with the English [language] in this country and that is the cant speech of the people. I know already several hundred words and write a short composition, but when I go out into the street and with wide-open ears follow every loud conversation, I don't understand a word of it for the Americans, Hyman says, never finish the word they begin and sometimes it occurs to me that I'll never learn to speak English.

The spelling and pronunciation are very hard and I was greatly amused several days ago when I went with Hyman to the public library to get a card—that the clerk asked me how to spell my name. In our country, I said, a girl who could not spell would not command such a position, but Hyman said that even the doctor, who cures his wife's rheumatism, asked him how to spell his name. Just think of it, the doctor, a university man, and cannot spell.

If there is anything that shows the standard of culture in a country or in a city — it is the public library system, and in this respect the United States, I think, leads the world. When I received my two cards, one for fiction and the other for non-fiction, made out for four years without a penny's expense on my part, I could scarcely believe it. I wondered much about it and asked Hyman how it is possible that no money deposit should be made. But the honorable Hyman, much elated in his heart at my astonishment (he being a great American patriot) answered that such is the "American style."

The public library, although not large enough for such a big city, contains a great number of books and journals and is well patronized. The thing surprising to me is that no policeman was there and whatever you do — you may be sure that no suspicious eye follows you. I noticed an old gentleman sleeping very comfortably over an open book, and another younger fellow, thinking that he is in his wife's bedroom, displayed his feet gracefully by placing them on the table in a very picturesque pose.

The American fashion of showing the feet more than the head irritates me often. In the streetcars all the men passengers before seating down perform a funny operation. They raise their trousers to a considerable height and evidently enjoy looking at one another's stockings and garters. I only wonder why the women should not adopt the same habit. It would prove a great success. Similarly, going out for a walk in the residence districts — I frequently notice a pair of limbs looking out from the window behind which the upper edge of a newspaper is seen. I conclude (and Hyman says rightly), that a head and the rest of the body is hidden behind the paper. Of course, it should be understood that the bodies of all these respectable readers rest on rocking chairs, for what a peasant's house at home [is] without vodka is an American home without rocking chairs.

Yes, this the country of rocking chairs and immensely large beds, for both of which I have the greater admiration. The American bed is so vast that a well fixed family, even with three pairs of twins included in the list of its progeny, would very comfortably accommodate itself in it, provided they lie crosswise. Where is the great patriot and benefactor of humanity, I query myself, who should undertake the importation of this article to our country, where such a blessed piece of furniture would be accepted with the eagerness that Israel showed towards the manna in the desert.

Talking about furniture — it is a very expensive article in this country, and the reason for it seems to be on the surface. The carpenters and the cabinet makers all over the United States enjoy an eight-hour labor day and get wages equivalent to the royal salaries received by the representatives in [the] *Duma* [parliament] in Petersburg [now Leningrad]. So, after all, some of the American workingmen do earn what our Socialists see in dream only, but, on the other hand, the high cost of living is very burdensome and the clamor of the masses is getting louder and louder.

My expectations that American edibles possessed different properties were positively groundless and people at home might change their minds about it. Although being antipodes, the skyscrapers and even the small buildings rest on the ground with their foundations and not with their roofs (to which my own eyes are witness). Just as well I found the American sugar not bitter, but sweet, and the milk white, if it is not watered (in the latter case somewhat blueish). The same refers to the butter, which sometimes changes its natural color, thanks to the inventive faculties of some American chemist. The eggs here are absolutely oval and if you possess that steadiness in your hand — they can be made to stand erect on either of its ends. As far as fishes are concerned — herring is not the only kind of them used here, and I found some of the thousands and one other sorts pretty tasty. The Americans, however, have to learn one thing in gastronomical matters from Russia, and that is manufacturing vodka, real, real strong vodka, for which the hearts of some of our country men here long so much, and, then, this country will reach the same degree as ours in one line of manufacture, for although genuine vodka is not to be found here, it is substituted by the other alcoholic drinks, and the number of saloons is so great that in this respect the United States beats Russia.

Kansas City, with a population of about three hundred thousand, has about four hundred and fifty saloons, which is, to my knowledge, the highest proportional rate in the world. Some of the streets are literally covered with them, and although a barefooted, ragged drunkard is an unknown sight here, you very often meet a nicely dressed gentleman, who looks like a "general in dismissal," and whose center of gravitation seems to have left its original position. If a drunkard of our country would meet his American colleague he would kneel before him and cross himself piously several times before addressing "his majesty." An American drunkard is usually a peaceful dove, and if he finds a dry, warm corner he will [be] content with resting there quietly. But the evil is the same everywhere and it is more disgusting to see it in a nicely dressed, civilized being than in a tattered, illiterate peasant. The statistics of this country show how enormous are the quantities of the liquor consumed. The people begin to realize the great harm caused by it and the prohibition movement is gaining ground.

The saloons are not the only pest in this country. Tobacco and chewing gum are the others. On every step you meet a pipe sticking from the mouth of a venerable citizen, a common pipe, at the look of which decent people at home would be horrified. And then the chewing gum. The other day I was riding with Hyman on a street car, and opposite us sat a young girl who was making queer motions with the muscles of her mouth. I was so amazed that for several minutes I gazed at her and wondered what kind of mouth disease she possesses. Hyman followed my look with knitted brows and kept quiet. I touched his shoulder with the hand and asked him for an explanation of this strange phenomenon. The expression of my face must have been very amusing, for Hyman suddenly burst out into such a wild, convulsive laughter that many a passenger was startled, a woman even screamed, thinking that her baby fell out through the window, and the conductor went up to us and looked at the violently shaking body of Hyman, who let out at equal intervals long, shrilling ha, ha, ha, hee, hee, hee. It is needless to add that the girl changed her seat immediately with a contemptuous look at us.

July 19 (?), 1914

One day last week I was alone in the house. Equipped with a dictionary, I was reading the history of Abraham Lincoln's childhood. A knock at the door interrupted my reading. In came a young American with a portfolio under his arm, and immediately making himself at home began to talk without waiting for any comment on my part. I understood nothing of his speech and resolved to tell him so. Slowly I composed a short sentence in my mind and still slower I pronounced it. I told him that I'm a foreigner and that I don't understand him. He seemed to be very much interested in me. He looked at the book I read and asked me a hundred questions in a simple language. I had to answer, and, of course, took great pleasure in making up my sentences and tried to use as many "high" words as possible. We chatted for half an hour, until finally he opened his portfolio and poured out a number of beautiful samples of different books. He was a book agent.

The benefit of my conversation with a real American was invaluable for me, because, strange as it might seem — it is a deplorable fact, that, while living in a typical American city in the heart of the United States,

I never yet had a chance to meet and converse with an American except in school, where conversation is given little time. The book agent praised my English so much and encouraged me to such an extent that I decided on the execution of a very adventuresome plan.

Without consulting Mrs. Hyman or even Hyman himself—who claims to be an expert on American affairs—I left the house and went to the biggest high school in town. On the way I considered every possible result of my enterprise. "There is no real danger," said I to myself, "if I'll not be accepted. Then, in the worst case, I might be driven out, but I'll not be arrested." Repeating again and again the last phrase I gained more and more boldness. But when I approached the large, majestic school building my heart sank within me and my firmness began to melt away so rapidly that when I was close to the door I became frightened and retreated quickly. Several times I repeated the same assault, but with the same result. I did not have the power to open the door.

Fortunately a man came out from the building and I confronted him in such a way that I had to enter. Once inside I went to the office and said "principal" to the clerk, meaning that I want to speak to the principal. I had composed the opening sentence of the conversation—"I want to learn"—but was still in doubt what word to use in it, "want" or "wish," thinking that the former is too harsh and commanding. I was shown into the private room of the principal. To my great surprise there was no lackey with shining copper buttons on the coat waiting at the door. In vain I looked around the room for a red-faced, angry looking, fat, uniformed principal. Instead I met the kind, inviting look of a neatly dressed, elderly gentleman sitting at the desk. He asked me what he can do for me. I told him that I *wished* to learn and, of course, pronounced it with such an accent that he at once understood what kind of student specimen he faced.

He motioned me to sit down, but I was so bewildered that I could not think of sitting in the principal's office. He asked me many a question and, in order to convince himself in the truth of my statement, he wrote down an algebraic formula and asked me to solve it. I did it immediately, but pronounced "$X2$" *eeks kvadrrat* (the first and second readers here contain very little algebra). I was accepted as a pupil in high school, and while waiting for my card I overheard the principal repeating *kvadr-r-r-at* to one of the teachers and they both had a good laugh over it.

It is very hard for me to get the correct American pronunciation of the letter "r"—and unfortunately this same letter is found in the most common word "all right," which very often causes me much inconvenience. The other day I was riding on one of the street cars and happened to stand on the rear platform. The conductor at one of the stops was collecting fares inside of the car and cried out to me the usual question, "All right?" I answered with such a shrilling "r" that it attracted much attention and resulted in a very sneering countenance of the conductor. Since then I try to patronize the pay-as-you-enter cars.

The inability to speak English embarrasses me greatly. I went yesterday to hear a famous sociological lecturer, and to my dissatisfaction I had on my left side one of those fellows who like to talk with everybody about socialism, anarchism, feminism and many other "isms." He soon turned towards me and made several remarks, which I did not understand. I had to say something, but knew not what and how, so I fixed my look at the ground and hoped that it might cleave asunder and swallow me as it did [the biblical] Korah and his followers in the desert.

The lecturer spoke loud and clearly and I understood most of his talk. The big hall was packed, but I was really amazed to discover while studying the faces of the audience that there were very few young boys and girls present. The younger generation in this great democratic republic is very little interested in social and humanitarian problems. It is a sad disappointment to the foreigner when he expects to find in the hearts of the present Americans the spirit of Franklin, Jefferson and Lincoln. Most of them look with contempt at the foreigner and sometimes very foolishly play tricks on him just because he happened not to know the English language.

When I go out into the street I find on the corners bunches of boys and girls, some of whom are high school and college students, who act very impudently. For hours they flock around the drug stores and jeer and mock at everybody. They never talk about anything else but sport and sporting seems to be the main thing in the life of this nation.

There is a game here called baseball, and everybody is talking about it everywhere. If a baseball player should chance to bruise his fingers all the newspapers would devote columns to it and some would even print extra editions and issue special bulletins hourly. But if a man like [the

British naturalist Alfred Russel] Wallace, perhaps the greatest thinker on earth, dies the same newspapers will occupy ten or twelve lines on one of its back pages. Of course, the daily paper here is a pure business establishment and delivers to the public the goods it demands.

Perhaps there is nothing so well characteristic of the American spirit as its newspapers. I believe it to be the greatest of the seven wonders of the world. The latest printing machines turn out more than one hundred thousand sixteen-page copies cut and folded. The price of the newspaper is one-fifth of the price at home — it is only one penny, and it is four or five times as voluminous as ours. But the Sunday paper beats them all in volume, in variety of material and in splendid arrangement.

What is known as the "yellow press" comprises the greatest part of the American newspapers. Many of them are used as tools in the hands of large capitalistic corporations and there is even one millionaire in the United States [William Randolph Hearst] who owns a dozen newspapers in the biggest cities in this country and he is a strong factor in politics. He influences millions and even founds parties through his papers. Of course, there are clean and decent newspapers, too, and Kansas City is fortunate enough to possess one of them. It reminds me of a great St. Petersburg newspaper, which always fights for the people, disregarding the many difficulties.

One at home would be surprised to know how soon the news reaches the public here. For instance, when [the czarist politician Peter Arkadievich] Stolypin was shot in Kiev on Thursday evening, the newspapers reached one at home on the following Saturday morning, while we knew it the same evening and even earlier than it took place, thanks to the favorable, for us, difference in time.

"Time is money," says Hyman, and in this country every minute seems to be worth something. When you go out into the business section of the city you see active people walking as fast as their feet can carry them. The workingman, says Hyman, who should be late on his job would be "fired." But just the same there is always an idle crowd in the streets and the slightest stop in the street traffic will draw a throng of jokers who will watch with the greatest interest a turn of a wheel or wink of the policeman's eye. The policeman here is the real servant of the public. He stands on the crossing of the busiest streets and regulates the traffic with a movement of the hand and with a whistle. I enjoy watching this work. Countless carriages, wagons, automobiles and street cars pass by him in the most admirable order under his directions. He never loses himself and never gets excited. In the midst of this babel of sounds and commotion he finds time to give the necessary information to a stranger or to walk over with an old woman from one sidewalk to the opposite, or to bring over across the street a baby carriage. And all this is done with the most polite and courteous manner.

Apropos the baby carriage. Hyman says that it is the pestilence of this country and often declares that he would have never come to the United States if he had any idea about it. And I don't blame him for it. Poor Hyman, every free moment of his time is occupied with the baby and its carriage. When he come to eat his hurried dinner — he always has to carry the carriage and the baby down from the third story where we live through the dark hall and the narrow stairs. In the evening, after a day of hard work, he never has a quiet supper, for Mrs. Hyman at every little noise or scream sends him down to look out for the baby. After supper the infallible task of carrying up the carriage through the same hall. On Sunday, the only free day in the week, Mrs. Hyman, very fashionably dressed with a golden chain on her neck and a heavy bracelet on each wrist, goes visiting. Before leaving she puts on the air of a suffragette and with a very militant look commands Hyman to take out the baby. The only consolation my venerable friend has is in the fact that many another husband is enjoying his sabbath in the same way and really by the time Hyman and the carriage (with the baby in it) arrive at the park — he finds all the benches occupied by husbands, mostly his friends, and the carriages lined up in numerous rows.

It happened not long ago on such a Sunday that Hyman, after a triumphal victory in a debate with the other husbands on the subject, "which is a better country, Russia or the United States" (Hyman invariably being on the side of the latter), it happened that he took a hold of another carriage (and, of course, of another baby, too) and brought it home. After supper he carried up the carriage and went to bed. It was about midnight when we were all awakened by an indescribable roar from Mrs. Hyman. In a moment the house was full of half dressed neighbors and lodgers. Mrs. Hyman was holding out towards the stupefied Hyman a dark little girl (it was Italian), whom she found instead of Mr. Hyman, Jr.

When Hyman recovered his senses he placed the baby in the carriage and went with it downstairs. In an instant an Italian woman, accompanied by some males, was at the place and threw herself at the baby and kissed and smacked it incessantly. Hyman began to worry about his own baby when two big smiling policemen with a baby carriage appeared from behind the corner.

Since that night Hyman began to long for his old country where millions are born every year and where people multiply and grow and live without baby carriages.

August 1 (?), 1914

I saw tonight the *Blue Bird,* by Maurice Maeterlinck. It was the first time I went to an American theater. The building was not very large, and the seating capacity was about that of an average Kiev theater. Outside, the structure does not look very artistic, but inside it is very well ornamented. The abundance of electric lights struck me here, too, and the splendid seats even on the balconies are certainly very agreeable. But the music was much worse than that of a very mediocre theater at home. The play itself was presented quite satisfactorily and the general impression was very pleasing, but I must confess that it is mostly due to the really excellent scenery. The trouble with the actors was that only two or three of them would deserve that name in Europe, while the rest were of a very talentless caliber. Hence, a contrast which sometimes is too conspicuous even to the average American theatergoer.

Of course the theater does not exist for the purpose of promoting art in this country; it is only a small link in a long chain of similar theaters scattered all over this country and owned by a company. It is purely a business establishment, and delivers the goods the public demands. However, it is said that this is the only place where you can see something classical and worthwhile. And very often these places are not well attended, when there happens to be in town a famous cabaret singer, for that is the kind of theater which is very popular here, and the number of these burlesque institutions in each town is astonishing. They are always full and prove a great financial success.

But that does not exhaust the public's passion for art. As a matter of fact, it is only a small percentage that does care for the theater. The greater part—and one at home would be amazed to know the vastness of this part—is enjoying the "moving pictures." While in our native land they prove quite popular, too, where they are already established, it would be a very poor comparison to draw any parallel between our and the American cinematographs. Technically, they are almost perfected here, and are vastly superior to ours. The greatest part of the pictures are nonsensical, but lately there is another class of pictures shown. The masterpieces of Hugo, Dickens [and] Scott and illustrated in a very vivid form, and the educational value of the pictures is becoming apparent. There is no doubt that in the near future they will be utilized on a larger scale for many valuable purposes.

It was Thomas Edison who invented the cinematograph, and it was he who perfected the telephone to a wonderful degree. I have finished reading today the latest biography of Edison, and it is from such a book that you see the marvelous country that the United States is. A poor boy from the woods, away from civilization becomes the greatest President of this republic and one of the mightiest and most illustrious humanitarian leaders. A newsboy becomes the greatest inventor of all ages and the benefactor of humanity all over the world. It is only by studying such characters that one can realize the opportunities found here, in the land of all possible impossibilities, or, as you call it there, "the golden land."

And if one wants to convince himself of the truth of this statement he should go out into the streets and watch the passersby. Their mouths are full of gold. What—the mouth? I see—you are stupefied, so was I, and in addition, I'll confess that I noticed it in Mrs. Hyman's mouth the first day, but was simply both afraid and ashamed to inquire. Those are the false golden teeth. There are very few people whose countenances are not decorated by these ornaments, and it is needless to say that it is of great value to many a young woman, both for its quality which enables her to display the gold as if it was a jewel and also for the opportunity it affords to come so closely in contact with a young dentist at the husband's expense. Yes, there is something the matter with the teeth in this country and Hyman authoritatively declares that the trouble is with the climate. "It is such a climate, you know," says he, "and that's all." And it is useless to argue, for Mrs. Hyman is always ready to put an end to the argument by reminding me that I'm "only a greenhorn."

The real cause is to be found in the food which is mostly not fresh. Everything here is monopolized and eggs stored for months, coming from China and all the other ends of the world, are sold for high prices. The public is standing it patiently and the newspapers describe with wonderful minuteness the royal calls of the "egg king." In Europe a country has only one sovereign, this land has many. There is a copper king, a steel king, a railroad king, a sugar king, a chicken king, a beef king, and many other kings. These kings are the real rulers of the country, and the pressure they exert on public opinion and life is a thousand times stronger than that of the czar. Here lies the answer to the question asked by many intelligent foreigners: Why is it that by gaining absolute political freedom they, however, feel themselves more slaves here than at home? But, as some Americans think, the foreigners are too philosophical, while the former are so busy that they don't notice why and how their natural teeth are being replaced by golden ones.

And perhaps the matter is much more simple than it seems. It is explained by an article which did not penetrate our uncivilized country. I mean the toothpicks. It is a simple, sharp little wooden stick that is called a toothpick in this country, and as the name tells you, it is employed by old and young, rich and poor, for picking the teeth. A table in a restaurant without a thousand toothpicks would be avoided as if it had no mustard on it, for they are both of importance to the American. We generally use mustard in medicine, but here a sandwich without mustard is what an *ukase* is without God. In short — an impossibility.

One can see that I'm becoming Americanized rapidly, for here I served you with something that is a puzzle to your mind. Don't imagine for a moment that a sandwich is a close relative to the world famous beefsteak. It is a slice of any "rotten" stuff carefully covered from your eye on both sides by two slices of bread, which, I'm sure, cannot be pierced through even by the strongest Roentgen rays. Such is the sandwich and its usual price is the renowned nickel.

It is the nickel that dominates this country, for pennies, although being in use and amounting to two kopecks, for which one can buy at home some fine breakfast, here these pennies are not in great honor, and if you are a [gentleman] your pocket will never defame itself by copper money. There are a thousand and one things one can get for a nickel and the most pleasant and entertaining is to see the "moving pictures." From my window, after supper, I watch satiated fathers and mothers and children standing in [a] row near the box of a nearby cinematograph and impatiently waiting for the turn to buy tickets. Mrs. Hyman is a frequent visitor there, too, but the worthy Hyman has to take care of the baby and his hands are always full of work. Mrs. Hyman also likes to spend her time in another interesting manner. In this city telephones are in great use and in all the drug stores its use is free. Well, Mrs. Hyman leaves Mr. Hyman outside to wait a while, she just wants to say a word to Mrs. Beinish, and once she takes a hold of the telephone there is no end to the conversation. Hyman meanwhile reads through (he is not a fast reader) all the titles of all the magazines in the window, then he passes to all kinds of soap and laxative medicines, then to some baseball bulletins of last year. Finally he loses his patience and peers into the drug store. Mrs. Hyman, thank heavens, is at the end of her conversation and is already saying good-by; but no, here she grasps the receiver again and "hallos" to Mrs. Beinish. She forgot to ask the most important thing; everything starts anew and the poor Hyman's brows become knitted, and it seems to me that he contemplates suicide.

Talking about suicides, they are not uncommon here and the news-papers devote little space to them, unless it be a more or less known personage's suicide. The causes are everywhere the same, and unhappy love claims a large number of them. On the other hand, you don't hear so often of suicides committed on account of loss of interest or meaning in life. People here don't look for a meaning in life, they take it as it is, and take it easy. Life is not a philosophical problem, not a puzzle to be solved in this country, but a strife among men with the object of gaining some more money. Rockefeller, Morgan and other financiers, who in Europe would be looked upon as enemies of the people, are here the idols, the very models placed before the growing generation. It is business that can be called the god of this country, and in all the schools business and not labor is pointed out as the ideal occupation.

The schools are not at all free in some states from a religious education, although the Constitution of the United States divorced the government from the church. The church, to my great astonishment, is greatly influencing the national life, although like everywhere it is mostly dead to the urgent problems of life. It is the same old story of napping audience and narrow-minded ministers in all denominations. But there are noble exceptions everywhere and some of the preachers already have left the books and "went out unto their brethren and looked on their burdens." These are extremely popular. The United States government fortunately is free from all religious influences and prejudices, and the officers belong to different denominations. As Hyman says, "Russia will change its form and shape a thousand times and undergo many a revolution, and then it won't be worth the finger nail of Uncle Sam."

Now, Hyman's patriotism, although absolutely genuine, is not at all unselfish. It happened that his name fell into the list of eligible jurors and it happened again that he was selected as a juror on a case of a pickpocket. Besides the three dollars a day which he received (and which are, of course, three dollars in currency), the honor bestowed upon him was too great a thing, and since then he believes himself and makes others believe that he knows all the secret policies of the government, and when there comes about a war with Japan [i.e., between Japan and Germany] Hyman's knowledge of strategies is wonderful; and the shoemaker downstairs frankly confessed to me that everybody in the street expects Hyman's appointment as United States ambassador to Turkey. It is understood that the Turkish ambassadorship is a rightful inheritance of our [Jewish] kinsmen since the days of Oscar Straus. In a word, Hyman is jubilant and meditative, and his look is full of importance and self-respect. Plainly he says: "Don't bother me!"

But Mrs. Hyman is very skeptical about the ambassadorship to Turkey, and when he returns home on Saturday afternoon and finds the two hands of Mrs. Hyman extended, not to embrace the future diplomat, but to take hold of the week's pay and verify the correctness of the amount; when he sees these hands, his clouded face betrays to me the fact that all the hopes for an Oriental family life are gone and that the militant feminism of Mrs. Hyman is becoming more and more tyrannical.

August 16, 1914

Today I had a very pleasant surprise in high school. The teacher selected from the pile of classes' compositions the one written by me and read to the class as a sample of good style. One can imagine the thrill of joy that ran through me—hearing the praise of the instructor. Of course, here it is not uncommon. The teachers in the American schools don't address their pupils by insulting nicknames, neither do they curse them for doing something wrong. The methods employed by the school faculty are quite different from those used in a Russian *gymnasia,* and the result is that the order and standard of knowledge attained in the classroom of the average teacher here are much higher than of those at home, where the military discipline in the schools results in an outspoken enmity between the teacher and the pupils.

The contrast between the life in the Russian and American schools is striking. Here it is not the aim of the faculty to suppress and to extinguish the sparks of individuality and idealism in the minds of the younger generation, but, on the contrary, to kindle and support them. The number of literary, scientific, social and art societies is astonishing and still more surprising is the fact that all these students' clubs are not persecuted by the police and not threatened with the imprisonment of their members, but are greatly encouraged and advised by the faculty.

The American elementary school may be called a palace in comparison with our institutions serving the same purpose. The spaciousness of the classroom, the splendid equipments, the cleanliness of everything within it, fully justify the use of this term. Its importance is hardly appreciated. There is no doubt that it contributed [immensely] to the building of this magnificent nation. It makes Persians and Irishmen, Africans and Caucasians, Germans and French, members of the American people. It defaces in a remarkably short period of time the harshest national characteristics and melts all the languages into one. While Russia, in itself composed of many nationalities, thinks that the best way to deal with them is the method of instigating one tribe against the other, of keeping them under the constant supervision of the Cossacks and holding them in ignorance. The achievements of the two nations tell which policy is the most successful.

When I was in Boston, a student of Harvard College took me over there to see the famous university. Before I reached the place I expected to see a huge building on the grounds, but I was greatly surprised. I imagined it to be something like the Kiev University, a vast red structure accommodating all the departments. Instead I found a whole town in itself; streets lined up with university buildings, professors' residences, students' dormitories and museums. In the library I found Japanese and Mexican students seated at the tables side by side with Americans and Brazilians. Generally, the cosmopolitan appearance of the public has a charm about it, that is at the same time very significant.

The American big city does not live one and the same life. The different nationalities have a very natural tendency toward flocking together, with the result that separate ghettoes, cities within cities, exist in the same towns. Each of these ghettoes is a world in itself, where only the native tongue is spoken and read. To the unobservant American it often appears to be a filthy stagnant pool; while, as a matter of fact, it is running water, always in the process of performing the great work of Americanization. Most of the immigrants, after a few years of struggle, succeed to such an extent that they leave the ghetto that witnessed their hard times to the newcomers, and move out into the more sanitary, fashionable residence districts. A good many of them buy there their own homes.

Now, in order to buy a house in this country, one must not necessarily have money. I know, Mrs. Hyman has already dispatched to you the news, that they bought a house worth twelve thousand dollars (which, of course, amounts to twenty-four thousand rubles). And I just see before me the wide-open mouths of the inhabitants of the whole town, when the astonishing news went around with the rapidity of lightning. "Hyman — a Rothschild!" is the general exclamation, and all his and her near and distant relatives must have left their work and have begun to wait for the next mail, which will bring them a pile of money orders. They will be bitterly disappointed.

Mr. Hyman invested in the house three hundred dollars. The first mortgage, held by the bank, amounts to nine thousand dollars. The second — held by a real estate firm — amounts to two thousand dollars and seven hundred dollars Hyman borrowed at a very high rate of interest from Mr. Bainish. The shoemaker downstairs, who is the best bureau of information in the whole street, told me confidentially that there is a rumor going around that the groceryman and butcher, whose stores are located in Hyman's building, lent to him a hundred dollars, which, added to the two hundred of his own, made the original capital. And so Hyman became a property owner.

And Mrs. Hyman is absolutely unrecognizable. From the early

morning her thundering voice makes the little children in the street tremble, and, when, accidentally, a huckster's wagon comes too close to the sidewalk, Mrs. Hyman sends an emergency call for the police. And I envy no longer the poor policemen, who never get less than three calls a day. The shoemaker says it is all "politics," and by a very knowing look he indicates that Hyman has some influence "higher up."

Recently I had an opportunity of seeing Hyman's relations with those people "higher up." I, accompanied by my worthy friend, went to the court to get my first naturalization papers, and when I had to declare that I drop forever my allegiance to the Russian Czar, Hyman gave vent to his patriotic feelings and exclaimed aloud, "Damn the czar," at which he received a look of contempt from the clerk. On our way home Hyman said that if "Abe" were there it would have been an entirely different case.

"Abe" is one of the political bosses of this city. One at home should not for a moment imagine that this great republic is really governed by the people. It is a political boss that holds the reins of the government in his hands; he is usually a saloon keeper or a person with a very dark record. Supported by a band of drunkards, he controls all the political jobs; by graft thousands of votes are purchased and the democracy of theory becomes a shameful despotism in fact. This kind of government in the city, as well as in the state, is tolerated by the people in the most amazing manner, and is looked upon as the natural order of things.

However, there is no pleasure greater than that of watching the crowds in the streets on an election night. All over this vast country the elections are held simultaneously, and the many meetings, demonstrations, parades and processions remind me that, after all, this is the land of freedom.

And Hyman says it is the land of presidents. This statement touches one of his great achievements. I mean — the presidency. For, on the very week when Wilson was elected President of the United States, by a remarkable coincidence Hyman was unanimously elected president of the Dry Goods Peddlers' Association. Yesterday he received a letter from a town in Russia, signed by several hundred persons, in which they appeal to Hyman, as to the President of this country, to shield them from the constant raids and aggressions of the czar's Cossacks. You can imagine how greatly Hyman was elated by the petition. For days he carried it in his upper pocket, exposing the end of the envelope with the foreign stamp on it. And to everyone in the street he read it over and over again. His prestige is growing by leaps and bounds, and Mrs. Hyman is indisputably the first lady of the street.

August 23, 1914

Several months have elapsed since I wrote you last. The winter — only a poor imitation of our winter — has passed and spring has come, enfolding the whole city in a cloak of green. This is my first spring in this country and I spend all my unoccupied time in seeing things. The city is now absolutely unrecognizable; it seems to me that it is the most beautiful of all the towns I have ever seen on either continent. Long streets and avenues — miles of them — are lined with thousands of trees, and when you look at them from an elevated place the town appears an enormous garden amidst the thick foliage of which beautiful green houses are hidden. There is nothing like it in our country, and only through the imagination can one get a picture in his mind of the wide, endless boulevards running through the city as the numerous veins in our body.

I closely inspected many of the private residences and apartment houses. They are charming architecturally, some of them imposing and majestic, others delicate and harmonious. However, a good many of them are red brick structures and at seeing these I invariably experience a feeling of aversion and disgust (their red color always reminds me of the Russian jails). In contrast to the beautiful residence section the business district lacks all sentimentalism. The main business streets in Vilna and Kiev are the sight of the town and are famous on account of the splendor of their buildings. Here the skyscrapers, built of iron and stone, solid like mountain rocks, stand erect like legendary demigods and defy art and aesthetics.

And if the skyscrapers are the symbolic embodiment of the driving power of this rich country — business — the churches are the true emblem of that semi-mysterious spirit which characterizes religion. The temples of prayer in this country lack the shining golden crosses on the tops of gilded steeples and cupolas and do not frighten the humble churchgoers with a strong and commanding facade, but gently captivate this soul with the earthly color of their stone and lead him out from the vanities of the world into their peaceful abode. As to the number of churches in this city, it can favorably compare even with Moscow, "the thousand-steepled." There are hundreds of them scattered all over the city.

But nevertheless, the morals in this country are not at all in an ideal state. The demoralization is great in almost every field of activity. The politician, candidate for county office as well as for governor and even for president, makes speeches everywhere in his own behalf, pointing out his virtues and making promises and giving pledges which he usually never fulfills. Some cheap newspapers publish news which is unreliable and false and attack decent citizens in the most outrageous manner. Some commercial and even educational institutions advertise themselves in the most shameless manner, declaring themselves the first in the country or in the world. One is amazed to read on every corner a sign announcing that here is located the largest and best emporium on earth. Then, the world-famous medical advertisements, that rob the honest simpleton of his hard earned dollar. Such professional charlatans establish themselves in some obscure corner and through the excellent mail service of this country reach the poor victim from the Atlantic to the Pacific.

And such a victim is Mrs. Hyman. She has already communicated with all the rheumatism "professors" in the states, but without good results. Three shelves of her bedroom closet are literally covered with all kinds of bottles and cans of different dimensions and contents, but Mrs. Hyman still continues experimenting. It is true that after getting disappointed by one of them she for a while abandons all hope and everything becomes quiet. But here Mrs. Beinish (a sister in distress) arrives with a newly received package (evidently her address is not unknown in some quarters) and everything is set in motion again. Now, the honorable Hyman is fully aware that it is another useless effort which will only cost him two months' rent that he derives from the shoemaker's shop, but this being the land of woman's supremacy, he deems it wiser to complain before me rather than before Mrs. Hyman. And I greatly sympathize with my worthy friend, who never fails to call my attention to the fact that "these are lucky days, for," he adds prophetically, "worse days are coming for man in this country, they (the women) will soon wear the trousers and we shall be dressed in skirts."

Such is Mr. Hyman's opinion, but Mrs. Hyman's brother, Joe, a boy of about 35 to 40 (estimates vary), is of an entirely different opinion on American women. It is his favorite subject and when once put on the track he runs along with such a tremendous power of eloquence that until the steam is out you can never halt him. In order to put him on that track one must only ask him why he does not marry. His eyes immediately light up, the yellow waxy face and sharp chin of a cunning insurance agent (that's what he is) betray an inner agitation, and the large mouth shows a tongue that will tire Mrs. Hyman, Mrs. Beinish and the grocery lady talking at the same time.

"The American girl, you know," he usually begins, "is a light minded, heartless creature, entirely ignorant of housekeeping, whose sole ambition in life are dresses, dances, chewing gum and chocolate." He goes on like that for quite a time and spares none of his knowledge on the subject for another time. Now, Joe's hostility towards the American girl is the result of a very sad experience of his. The shoemaker tells me that when the scandal happened the "world was going round" and that even the pictures were in the papers. In this country if you see a fire and call for help you will immediately have the honor of seeing your picture under a crying headline that you saved the whole city from destruction. Of course, when the fire happens late at night and you jump out of bed you must avoid the camera of the reporter, who is never too careful on such occasions. Well, poor Joe had a girl, and she, after the American fashion, sued him for $10,000 for an alleged breach of promise. Here, if a boy takes a girl to a park once or twice and then shows lack of interest in her, he may be sure to receive a letter from a lawyer informing him that a case has been started against him. The newspapers are full of such cases and they occupy leading places on the front page.

But although Joe dislikes the American girl, I must say that he is not at all right. I have some interesting statistics to show in her defense — provided you rely on my taste in this matter. It was last week, while passing by a high class theater at the time when the spectators, mostly women, left the building, that an idea struck me, the execution of which I undertook at once. I stood near the doorway and counted the passing women, taking special notice of the beautiful ones. The result was astonishing; out of forty-eight women I thought fourteen were pretty. It seems to me to be a record breaking number, and, although the American girl lacks the dark, fiery eyes or the coal-black hair of some European beauty, she gains in gracefulness and in stature.

But Mrs. Hyman, who still considers herself an extraordinary beauty, hates to hear compliments paid to some girl in the presense of Hyman. She is always on the lookout and thinks (one need only look at her for a moment in order to see that she is not wrong in her thoughts), that the faithful Hyman contemplates leaving her and that he carefully plans an elopement after the American fashion. Now, these thoughts are absolutely groundless, Hyman being the staunchest supporter of the institution of marriage in the whole street (he is a great admirer of Theodore Roosevelt). But Mrs. Hyman does not believe in the steadiness of political principles, and her watchful eye is always awake to take proper care of her beloved "bread giver."

August 30, 1914

The long feared American summer has finally come, but as you say it over there, "the devil is not so black as he is painted." In fact, the stories about hundreds of heat prostrations have fortunately proven to be wild exaggerations and I find the climate here during the summer very similar to the one in Southern Russia, as in Ekaterinoslav [now Dnepropetrovsk], or even in Kiev, with the only exception that we don't have here such violent storms as in those provinces.

However, as fine as the climate here may be, it cannot compensate me for the one great disappointment I had with the famous Mississippi River. Full of Mark Twain's vivid descriptions of the river, I expected to find something like the Dniepr or Volga, wide, swift and limpid, but I was soon disenchanted. Here it is not generally used as a bathing place, and in the few small bathing places I saw a most surprising and amusing sight — men and women bathing together. Of course, that will astound you, but what is more astounding is the fact that the bathing persons wear special suits, and how ridiculous and funny it was to me to see a woman dressed from head to foot in a suit that seemed hardly less comfortable than that of a diver just for the purpose of bathing in the company of men.

But these bathing suits should not for a moment suggest to you that the American shuns water and therefore is not clean. It would be a gross mistake. The cleanliness of the American people is rightly a subject of envy by every civilized foreigner; it seems that being clean to the American is a natural inborn thing and not an art. I wish that instead of being taught English first, the newly arrived immigrant should be in some way or other instructed or even forced to keep clean his home, the street and his business establishment. It is astonishing to see the difference between the immigrants' district and the one inhabited by the American workingmen. Of course, it is foolish to criticize the former, when it is considered that the majority of the foreigners, crowded in one small district, come from all the corners of the earth, each group with its specific customs and traditions, and in addition, most of them from the poorest and most oppressed classes in their respective native lands. It is a fact that the average American is blind to all this, and hence the contemptible look at the foreginer, who in many cases proves to be superior to the native.

The American fails to appreciate in most cases the good done to this country by the foreigner. When I was in the East I built up in my mind a theory (which fortunately has proven false) that this country is entirely in the hands of a plutocracy. This was based on mere observation; wherever I went, whatever I watched, I found that the foreigners do the hard work. In vain I searched in New York and Boston among the thousands of subway laborers for a genuine American face. I found it only in the person of the foreman with charts and plans in his hands. It was the same in the construction of bridges, in the mines and in the mills and factories. "The Americans," a friend told me in Boston, "are the clerks, salesmen, engineers, doctors, politicians and business men," the ones who profit by the foreigners' labor and who at the same time cry and shed crocodile tears about the "foreign invasion."

So much for the city. In the country, fifty miles from Boston, a most beautiful spot, where our friend B. has just bought a farm, I found positive proofs of the degeneracy of the "Yankee." Farms, bearing the signs of former prosperity and even splendor, are now in a shattered and neglected state and are on sale for half of their value. I once passed by an abandoned house, and in response to my inquiries I was told that the farmer had two sons, one a lawyer in Boston, and the other a student at Harvard, and not being able to cultivate the farm himself, which by the way was all drowned in mortgages, he had to move into the city and leave it in the hands of an agency. Such examples are numerous in the East and they certainly show what valuable service the immigrants render to this country.

After all, the fact remains that this country is primarily a land of immigrants, and that beginning with the pilgrims and ending with the persecuted Jew, the millions of immigrants that came to this country have never failed to contribute all the best that their body and soul had to the building of this magnificent nation. It seems to me that the average American is much less appreciative of the American liberties and consequently less patriotic than the average Americanized foreigner. I do not doubt for a moment that in case of need the hundreds of thousands of foreigners who came to this country from Europe in order to escape the severe military service, would at the first call to arms at once volunteer to serve under the Stars and Stripes, and cheerfully die for this country which they adore so much. There is something in the American state and federal institutions, something in the spirit by which they are taking care of the people that is so dear, beloved, parental to the immigrant, that is much stronger than the bonds binding him with the [European] fatherland; stronger even than all the deep religious and nationalistic tendencies that yet connect him with the recent past.

The reason for this is on the surface. Take, for instance, the way the city government is taking care of the people. Did you ever hear at home that a citizen should know anything of what the city authorities are doing for him? The citizen must pay the taxes, if not a policeman or two will introduce him to a Russian jail; but how those taxes are expended no one knows. It is quite different here. Besides the splendid schools that the city furnishes for the children, the city is doing something which will sound incredible to you. It is taking care of these same children after they leave the school buildings. It provides them with playgrounds in different sections of the city and these playgrounds are not empty, but equipped with everything required to give the children a good time and at the same time to develop them physically. Tennis courts, municipally owned bathing places and numerous other things foster in the hearts of every growing citizen a feeling of love, loyalty and pride that is absolutely unknown in our country. It is this loyalty and pride that brought about the magic growth of such cities as Chicago and Kansas City. The natural resources and geographical location could not have accomplished so much without the spirit of the American citizen.

Here every city claims to be the first in something. Every city, whether it has a population of a million or of a thousand, points with pride to some achievement which is said to be the best, or the most famous in the whole country. If you express unfavorable opinion about a town to one of its citizens, he will consider it more offensive even than a personal insult. Statistics are always at hand, the latest and the most reliable, to prove that in a year or in a century the city will have so many inhabitants and so many factories. The street urchin as well as the banker are always ready to defend the honor of their city with their fists, for, if you still remember the [Jim] Jeffries-[Jack] Johnson fight [held at Reno, Nevada, in 1910], about which you read in the newspapers, you will also recollect the riots by which it was followed, which is a good proof of the American's fighting spirit.

However, as much as the Americans are such experts in fighting, there are a number of things in this country that they seem to lack the interest to fight against, and, I believe, the most important thing is the vice problem. It is a disgrace to this country to endure conditions that are much more terrible than in Russia, and the most deplorable fact about these conditions is the indifference of public opinion and the silence most of the newspapers maintain on this subject, the result of which is an indirect support of these conditions. It is this "modesty" that irritates me, as if the best way to cure a disease is to ignore its existence, and when you read in the paper that a judge fined a young man $100 or three months' imprisonment for writing a note to a girl, or that one must pay $5,000 for a kiss, you might think this is the land of the ideal moral life. But the thousands of elopements, divorces and "alimony" cases tell a frightful story of a bankrupt morality.

Hypocrisy is the chief characteristic of the capitalistic society, but Hyman, the capitalist, thinks otherwise. "It's all, you know, the unions," says he. "They make all the trouble; I would give them the electric chair and be done with them." This sudden change in Hyman's political and economical teachings is due to the fact that he has become a "waist manufacturer."

September 13, 1914

The school season has begun, and by taking a few extra examinations I "skipped" a year and am now in my third year. All my teachers were astonished at the improvement in my speech, which is due to the fact that during the vacation months I worked in a large department store where only English is spoken. All that I accumulated in theory during the winter months underwent a practical test this summer and proved to me that the knowledge I gained in school was invaluable. However, the knowledge I acquired while working was not less important, for I came in contact with the American employee and employer and learned their relations.

Of the fifteen persons employed in the department I was working in, only two treated me like their equals, and were very friendly towards me all the time. The behavior of the rest was unspeakable. Just because I am a foreigner and cannot speak English as well as they (that is my only crime), I was the object of continuous insults and foolish tricks on me every day of the week. I was the scapegoat on all occasions and whenever there was some extra work to be done after the closing hours, or whenever there happened to be something hard to be accomplished, I was always ordered to do it. Nevertheless, I was always confronted with the statement that foreigners don't like to work hard, which is, of course, a deliberate lie.

The sorry side of this incident lies in the fact that all these fellows were not illiterate peasants (although they acted like ones), but were educated in the schools of this country. It plainly shows that something is the matter with the schools; that, although they succeed in equipping their students with bookish knowledge (although they provide them with nice diplomas and very often with positions), they fail to equip them with that respect for man and with that love for your neighbor which should make them realize that they are members of humanity ever striving toward the ideal. One can find numerous proofs to the effect that the American school needs a reform which should change the character of the people (ultimately). That such a change is necessary no one will dispute, considering these interesting facts.

You have doubtless heard about lynching on the other side of the Atlantic. But it is different to pick up a newspaper one morning and to find somewhere in its interior an obscure item telling of a whole town surrounding a prison and, after breaking into it, lynching a prisoner, who sometimes happens to be a woman. Such outrages, which happen very seldom in the most obscure villages in Siberia, are committed here very often in the sunny daylight in towns where splendid school buildings tell of civilization and culture. In most cases the guilty go unpunished and the newspapers representing public opinion pass on it as a matter of course. This is the most amazing part of such occurrences.

But still more surprising to the immigrant who expects to find the living spirit of Jefferson are the numerous cases of capital punishment. The country that produced the sewing machine, the telegraph and the telephone, had also produced a guillotine of the twentieth century, a "humane" electric chair. Instead of a bloody convict-executioner, a civilized college graduate does the work. And that terrible story of Leo Tolstoy in which he describes that vampire-hangman who feared daylight can hardly apply to his American colleague, who after accomplishing his work enjoys an excellent luncheon at the City Club in the company of the most enlightened citizens. "You see, we live," says the American, "in a highly cultured age, and we can just as well afford to have a decent-looking executioner of the law."

The law! Can there be anything more cynical than the way it is interpreted in this country? The Thaw case is the best illustration of what I mean. A horde of well paid lawyers, backed by millions, have outraged the first constitution in the history of mankind. The trusts, employing the best lawyers in the country, defy the law and the nation. The state and federal parliaments are full of trust representatives who betray the people. The political bosses have in their hands thousands of positions for distribution to their assistants in compensation for purchased votes. The police, as it has just been proved in New York, are protecting vice and gambling places and the number of crimes in this country is appalling. Everything is politics, and the welfare of the people is sacrificed to personal ambitions everywhere.

Is there anything more comical than the fact that as soon as a new President from another party is elected hundreds of thousands of jobs filled by experienced employees become the prey of the new party and an army of inexperienced politicians fill the antechambers of the bosses waiting for their turn? Isn't it ridiculous to see the craze of some state legislatures to create new laws in most astounding rapidity, laws which are valid only on paper? The Massachusetts legislature recently made a law forbidding the use of long hatpins. This law had no effect at all and is not even generally known, while there is a constant clamor from the masses for important legislation, a clamor which is somehow ignored.

The masses, of course, are the laboring people, and they play already a very important role in the life of this country. The labor question is on the *Tagesordnung* [agenda], and many Western states, the more radical of the [Federal] Union, are dealing seriously with this problem. The unions are a positive factor in the national life and the voices of their leaders are heard all over the country. Some of the states went even as far as acknowledging the benefit of state ownership and, strange as it is, it is a fact that at the same time when the climax of capitalism is reached in many branches of industry, seeds of socialism are being planted under the legal protectorship of the government. This affirms my belief that this country will one day proclaim a new Declaration of Independence intended for mankind all over the earth.

But if the lawyers and the law have not served this country honestly, the medical men have and continue to serve humanity most devotedly. The fame of the American surgeon is not at all overestimated. The wonderful operations they accomplish sound almost incredulous. One reads often of restoring sight, or of saving a person's life, thanks to the audacity and skill of the physician. The American hospitals are superb in every respect and are incomparably higher than ours. The medical schools in this country are numerous and some of them enjoy a universal reputation. Altogether, there are five hundred colleges and universities of every description in this country while there are not more than twenty-five higher educational institutions in Russia, which has a much larger population than the United States. That shows how far behind we are at home and it will take centuries before Russia will in any way approach this country.

And if there is anything in which the difference between the two countries is striking it surely is the barber shop. An American barber shop in no way resembles our establishment answering the same purpose. When you enter a barber shop here it is not only for the purpose of taking a shave and a hair cut, but you may as well enjoy a bath (don't worry, there is a laundry office at hand) and then also a shoe shine. But that is not all; in some places there is a pool hall in back and a saloon at its side where the customer is afforded the opportunity of having a good time. Hyman once had a very sad experience in such a barber shop. He had stretched himself royally on the red plush throne and was thinking about the real pleasure one can get for a quarter when he became so transported that to all the questions of the barber he answered "yes." Well, after enjoying the gentle administrations of the barber for an hour he had to pay $1.25 for a massage and many other things, the names of which he did not know. Indeed, after this operation he looked very young and blooming and Mrs. Hyman met him with a celestial expression on her face (at which he was greatly pleased, let me tell you), but just the same he began to denounce the unions in still more forcible terms, declaring them to be "bands of robbers."

The barber shop is not the only distinguished establishment differing from ours. Here you find something unknown in your places. I mean the manicuring parlors. I once stood for several minutes near such a place, watching a young, lovely girl manicuring an old fellow. It was a sight worth seeing, at the same time reflecting an interesting light on American habits.

Picnics, camps and outings for children were very numerous during the summer and there are many societies taking care of the poor boys and girls. It might be disputable if charity work is the right cure for poverty, but there can be no doubt that these institutions are organized wonderfully and the philanthropic work in the country is so extensive that the number of national organizations is very large. An interesting feature of it is the fact that the needy and destitute immigrants are well taken care of by their respective kinsmen. If not for these organizations the city government would have its hands full of work, and it must be said here that the average American appreciates this work very little.

In many cases this work is connected with the religious congregations, each church taking care of its members. The worthy Hyman has lately become an ardent church-goer and all the members of the congregation have the deepest regard for the "waist manufacturer." The shoemaker, who belongs to the same synagogue, told me yesterday that the election of the president is approaching and that he has positive information that Hyman "has an eye on the chair." The near future will show whether Hyman will occupy this high position or not, but one thing is certain to all the "landspeople" [the people from the same district in Europe], that Hyman's ambitions are unlimited. He is rising higher and higher to the great delight of Mrs. Hyman, who celebrates each new direction by adding a new plume to her already gorgeous bonnet.

September 27, 1914

Today is the second anniversary of my being in this country. Two years ago I stepped on American soil with a feeling of awe and respect for the New World; now this awe has become admiration and then respect — worship. Time has had its effect, and in the great "melting pot" I, among many thousands, underwent the same process of Americanization. I am not as yet what I want and hope to be, but your life (Russian) is no longer my life nor your country mine. I will no more speak about Russia in my letters as of my home, for I found a new and better home here under the American flag. I have been here only two years and I am sorry I did not come over some years before, so that I would now be a citizen. As it is I have to wait three more years, and I am anxious that these years should pass as quickly as possible.

I notice that I stopped thinking in my native tongue, but do it now in English, which is a sign that I finally succeeded in mastering to a certain extent the language which seems to be the hardest of all the European languages. I also had an essay on Benjamin Franklin published in one of the American newspapers and you can imagine how greatly I was elated by it. I am doing a lot of reading, and you would be surprised to learn how little real literature there is in the United States.

The five writers who are widely known abroad, I mean Hawthorne, Poe, Longfellow, Mark Twain and Jack London, are really the only ones who deserve the names they bear. Of them only three are typical American writers who were little influenced by foreign literature. As to Poe and Longfellow, even American critics agree that their creations are more European than American. However, there is such a thing as American literature, a literature which will live and bear that stamp forever, be it only due to Hawthorne's *House of the Seven Gables* or to Mark Twain's excellent works, which are distinctly American. Jack London, who was becoming so popular in Russia when I was about to leave the country, although so young and promising, has already reached the zenith of fame and like Maxim Gorky is playing the role of a "retiring general." There is a great similarity between the American and Russian writers mentioned, and I don't doubt that the future historian of the world's literature will find an interesting parallel running between Gorky and London. Both have risen from the "hobo" to the position they hold now [and] added new vigor, new blood to the body of literature. Gorky has given us the scent of a fat, black fertile soil, London the odor of a vast, breezy ocean. Both Gorky and London speak of the world boldly, freely and directly. And finally, both are very popular.

The backbone of American literature is English, and the libraries would almost become empty if the works of the English should be withdrawn. All the English classics were expropriated by the Americans and Shakespeare has become at home in this country as well as in his native land. The same is true about Dickens, Scott, Kipling and the rest. As a matter of fact, in all the schools of the country they are being studied as classics and that helps greatly in solidifying that feeling of kinship which exists between this country and Great Britain. It is an excellent proof of what a language can accomplish.

But if America is striving for a place on the literary Parnassus and is evidently not far from its goal — it is still very much behind in art. I don't mean the art of money-making, for the latter is developed here as in no other country on earth. I meant the so-called "fine arts." It is true that the American millions buy annually the best productions of the old and modern European masters; it is also true that the museums in New York rank among the best in the world and that the Metropolitan Opera House is the first on earth, but that is not due to great native talent, but to imported "stock" which is being paid in heavy gold.

However, there is a great awakening in progress and those thousands of Americans flocking to Italy, France and other European countries to study and perfect themselves in art, will bring new minds to their fatherland and it may be safely said that healthy seeds of an independent typical American art are being planted on this soil which has already proved to the world its fertility. In a generation or two, I believe, the country that has given the world a Wright and an Edison, will also give it a Sarah Bernhardt or Caruso. The phlegmatic Englishmen contributed that matter to the body of the American people which gave the world the great American inventors. Now the turn comes for the Italians and Russians to prove that what they bring to this country is not waste but light. It is their task to produce the great artists, and I do not doubt for a moment that this task they will fulfill most gloriously. I would say to the present American: "Wait, give those Italians and Russians their time!"

You, in Europe, know too well that the industrial unrest that is fermenting in all the civilized countries, is not a local issue but an international one, that it cannot be helped by one nation and that it is a clear prediction that a great change is to take place in the social system of mankind in the future. The best illustration of what I mean is the constantly increasing apprehension of the wealthy classes in Paris of a popular uprising against them.

Now Paris has no immigration problem; on the contrary, the thousands of tourists pour into pockets of the Parisians millions of dollars every year and yet the suffering of the poor is terrible there and the question of unemployment is as acute in Europe as in the United States. But here God blessed the country with immigrants, and the American, let me tell you, most foolishly lays all the trouble the country has at the door of the poor immigrant. The American does not want to see that the industrial unrest is not a result of immigration, but of unspeakable conditions existing here. The American does not want to turn to his own history and see that panics occurred in the United States in times when the current of immigration was very small. I refer to the panic following Jackson's administration. But even in those days the politicians found a "scapegoat," which is still serving them as an amazing instrument to fool the people on election days. I mean the tariff.

For more than a century the "tariff" has been made the main issue of the leading political parties. Thousands of volumes have been written, half of the standard school history is full of the "tariff," and millions of votes were cast for and against it. The tariff was always at hand as a remedy for the troubles of the country, a remedy which has always failed, for the cost of living is rising, despite the fact that not a single president of the United States has not had his hands full of the "tariff." It has been the tariff up and the tariff down alternately, but with no substantial result. And just the same the American is being fooled the same old way.

January 31, 1915

Three years ago, when I was spending my evenings over the first and second readers desperately, struggling with the queer spelling of "knife" or with the pronunciation of "through," I had not even dreamed of the possibility of my becoming some day an instructor of the "hardest of languages." This was the name I gave to the English tongue. "Why," I used to say to my Americanized friend John, "here is a language that has the most gigantic dictionary of all languages of the world," pointing to the Webster's Unabridged, "and it has no grammar at all. Take, for instance, the pronunciation. Now how in the world could one ever learn it when 'gh' in one word is pronounced like an 'f,' in another word like a 'g' and in the third one it is not pronounced at all. Or, take that d—d letter 'w,' the teacher says to me: 'you must protrude the lower lip forward.' Well, here we came to the word 'water.' I read 'votter,' the teacher says 'no.' Then I stuck forward my lower lip and said 'pfoder.' She says 'no.' Then I open my mouth and say 'vooder.' But here again she says 'no.' Then I became indignant and sat down, saying to Miss Stone: 'That's no language, English.'"

As to the spelling, even John had to agree that it was barbarous. At first he was stubborn on this point also. "Wait," he would say, "you will get used to it and you will think otherwise." Now this irritated me. "What do you mean?" I once asked him, "Do you mean to tell me that when we two went to the postoffice to send fifteen rubles home and that clerk asked me how to spell my name, mind you, my name, you mean to tell me that this English language is a language? No sir, if a United States officer cannot spell my name, then this language is rotten." In vain did he try to convince me that it was impossible for a person to learn the spelling of names of different nationalities, I would not listen to him. But in justice to John it must be said that he soon acknowledged that I was right. It happened thus: He came across a story in a newspaper about a spelling contest that was conducted among school teachers. Now that alone was an argument in my favor. A spelling contest among teachers! Who ever heard of anything [like it] in the Old Country? Among the three hundred contestants there was not a single one who could spell correctly all the given words! And, moreover, the best of the bunch, a principal of a country school, flunked on the spelling of the word "acquiesce." "Here you are," I exclaimed to John, "either the teachers are not teachers or the language is no language."

Well, that was three years ago. It must be understood that all these heated arguments I used to have with John were put up in my native tongue, for, as I used to say then, I was "as dumb as a fish" when it came to conversing in English. No, I would not speak English, I said to myself many a time. It is true that I know more words than many fellows who are already "talking," but as soon as I open my mouth there is always a "w" in the way and I have to protrude my lower lip, and if I am lucky enough to escape the "w" by a flank movement, well, there is no way of evading the cursed "th" which I have learned to hate even more than the "w," for the simple reason that while there is no danger in opening your mouth and sticking forward your lower lip, there is a grave danger in the "th," danger of biting your own tongue. After having bitten my tongue more than once, I decided to give up all hope of ever learning to pronounce "th" right. But now I am teaching them to bite their tongues.

"Mr. Lippman," I said, "please read the first word in that column."

"That column " was a special "th" column I had prepared for the evening.

Mr. Lippman looks at me with his dark eyes as if praying for mercy. "Take pity," says his look; "my tongue has not healed yet from last week's exercises, take pity." But I am merciless, nay brutal. The voice of revenge within me urges me on to avenge the tortures I had three years ago. I want satisfaction, it is plain, and I am going to get it. Yes, my friends, it is your turn now. You have escaped from the Cossack's whips or from military service in the czar's armies, but there is no way of escaping that "th," believe me. I put on an air of an executioner and say:

"Mr. Lippman."

The poor fellow has already put in motion all the muscles of his throat and mouth, one can see that, but still without result. Finally I hear:

"D-d-d-d-d."

And then comes:

"D-d-toid."

The word on the blackboard was "third." I knew the hardship of pronouncing the "th" itself, but I wanted satisfaction, and so I added the "ir" to it. The "ir" and the "th" made a good combination for causing the tongue [to] slip in between the teeth. That was all I wanted.

Mr. Lippman could not continue. I saw it by the expression of pain that appeared on his face.

Another "character" in my class is Mr. Ziablikofsky. He has his ideas about things, one can see that. It was a short time ago that we had our first lesson in geography. The map of the world looked fascinating to most of the pupils. Here they come up to it and find Kansas City in one place, Vilna or Warsaw in another place, and right there is Bremen, the [German] port from which they left Europe, while pretty close to Kansas City is Galveston, the place where they first landed in this country. But Mr. Ziablikofsky is not like the rest. He does not believe in the roundness of the world. You can see in his eyes a defiant statement. "No, you don't fool me!" is what it amounts to.

At first I did my best to convince him that the world is round. I invited him to see me before class and after class, and made use of my eloquence in all the languages of the world, including that of gesticulation, all with the purpose of convincing Mr Ziablikofsky that the world is round. But it was all useless. He was not moved from his original argument. "If the world is round," he says, "it must be round, but why is it flat? Noo, why is it flat?" he closes emphatically. Now go and talk to him! I would like to see that person who could make Mr. Zalmoon Ziablikofsky believe that the world is not flat, but round. Of course, you could read to him a lecture about it every night, but every night you will also read in his distrustful, suspicious countenance the defiant statement, "No sir! You won't fool me!"

———

Isaac Don Levine, who was born in Byelorussia in 1892, came to the United States as a young man of nineteen, spent some time in the Midwest and in New England, and ultimately became well known as a writer and journalist, the author of books about the Russian Revolution and Soviet leaders like Lenin, Stalin, and Trotsky, as well as American notables like General William Mitchell and Mervin K. Hart. Between July 5, 1914, and January 31, 1915, the Kansas City Star *published Levine's letters supposedly written to relatives in Eastern Europe. The letters, as the editor of the* Star *said, "give an interesting insight into the viewpoint of the newly arrived immigrant of culture and education." Reprinted here (with some deletions), they retain the occasional malapropism and a general quaintness of expression which were used by Levine as humorous attempts to portray the Jewish immigrant's "struggle" with the English language.*

New York's Lower East Side, 1905

Growing Up on the East Side

Ida R. Feeley

y father was born on March 4, 1870, in a small town in the Carpathian Mountains in Rumania. His father did not believe in naming children after a deceased relative, but preferred naming the infant after some great hero in the Bible, so the name picked for him was *Hillel*. His mother thought the name too much for a little boy to live up to and so called him *Hillick*. His parents conducted a store where they sold food and wine and were able to raise their children in an Orthodox environment. The children went to *cheder* and lived a normal life according to the times. The family got along with the non-Jews and always knew in advance when an uprising would occur. My father attended school and could read and write Rumanian as well as Hebrew and Yiddish.

This was a resort town where the Rumanian king and his family visited for health reasons, drinking the mineral waters and bathing to cure their many ills. My father often in his talks about his home town recalled the Russian army marching through the town on their way to fight the Turks and buying black bread with *brinza* (salty cheese) and caviar and wine: they paid gold coins for the repast. Also popular was the corn bread *(momaliga)* and cheese.

My father stated that, according to the Bible, war was always going on and peoples were conquered and enslaved and there would never be an end to war. He said that the ten tribes of the Jews had disappeared but that they were apparently settled throughout the world. He enjoyed listening to the *chazanim* who chanted songs from the Bible and he would attend the synagogue on the High Holidays if a well known cantor was going to participate in the service.

When my father grew up, he was physically strong and was a merchant. He was a hard worker and drank wine with his meals. He was interested in helping his fellow man in need.

When he was twenty-six years of age, he was introduced to my mother, Chova Liebowitz, the daughter of a man who owned a pottery and china dish factory. She had been educated by tutors and spoke and read Rumanian, French, Italian, Russian, Hebrew and Yiddish. She was the bookkeeper for her father's business. A matchmaker had arranged the marriage, and since the parents were mutually pleased with the match, the two young people were married and as part of the dowry continued to live with her parents. My brother was the only child born in Rumania and was brought to the United States as an infant in arms. He was named after my mother's father Wolf (William).

My father found that times were hard and that he could not make a living on his own. Enticed by the glowing letters that he received from his sister Esther Cohen, who emigrated with her husband Joseph Cohen to America, he decided to arrange to emigrate too.

When my father arrived in New York City, he saw a horse and carriage, hailed it and drove in style to his sister's address, a four-room flat on the East Side, where he was received with great joy. He apparently lived with his sister's family and started to save money for the arrival of my mother and their son. He obtained employment as a wine maker and hired a pushcart for the sale of merchandise on the streets of the East Side.

In due course my mother and brother arrived from Rumania and were established in their own four-room tenement apartment consisting of a kitchen, two bedrooms and a living room. The toilet was in the hall and was used by two families, so a supplementary potty was available for emergencies.

Because her neighbors were ignorant gossips, my mother did not get along with them. My mother was anxious to learn the English language. With her education she was able to earn a few pennies in reading the letters that neighbors received from their families in the Old Country. She also wrote replies for these people. I remember her reading letters and crying together with her clients and rejoicing at good news. My mother wrote to her brother asking him to emigrate so that she would not be alone in America without family.

I know that we lived at several addresses on the East Side and that I was born on First Street on Passover eve, April 4, 1904. My two sisters were born in the bedroom of 104 Norfolk Street and were delivered by a midwife. Doctors were available, but most of the women preferred the services of a midwife.

As soon as a family arrived in the United States, relatives arranged for the father to join a fraternal lodge, which provided a doctor and burial ground in the event of death in the family. The doctor took care of the entire family for a very slight fee.

There were very few labor unions and free enterprise was the only source of supply and demand. The chief market place was Orchard Street, which had several stores and pushcarts along the entire street. The groceries had a credit system which covered purchases for the week and when the workers were paid by their employers they would settle their accounts.

I remember buying hot *obas* [*sic* — probably *arbas*, chickpeas] and sweet potatoes and knishes on the East Side; also delicious delicatessen sandwiches and kosher pickles. In the summertime my father would purchase a whole watermelon from the carts and slice it up for the family and our next door neighbors to enjoy.

Our apartment consisted of four small rooms, a kitchen, two bedrooms and a living room. My brother slept on a couch in the living room. It was a cold water flat with gas fixtures. Later it was electrified and all hot water was heated on the kitchen stove, which was stuffed with wood from my uncle's shop or occasional coal. A bath was taken once a week in a tin tub on the kitchen floor or in the kitchen washtubs. As we became older we went to the city shower bath facilities and stood in line with our soap and towels. I also went to the Turkish bath with my Aunt Sarah where I received a real scrub-down and was abashed by the nakedness of the women. My mother had a first cousin, who was a real friend, and since her husband was a waiter they were able to live in Harlem and had a private bath. My mother would take the four children to Harlem on a Saturday morning and we were all bathed and enjoyed a pleasant day with her cousin.

In the summertime the family slept on the roof or on the fire escape attached to each apartment in order to catch some breeze and avoid the terrific heat. Everyone slept in their underwear, as nightgowns and pajamas were considered luxuries. Some of the more affluent tenants went to the *kuch-alain* (housekeeping cottage) country places in the Catskills for a week or two and were the envy of the people who stayed home.

The residences on the East Side were known as tenement houses and were full of rats, vermin, cockroaches and bedbugs, which could not be entirely eliminated as they were in the walls, pipes and cracks of the building. Every household maintained a cat which was both a pet and protection against the mice and rats. Setting traps was of no use. The Board of Health and the city inspectors did nothing about these conditions. I know that my mother applied all sorts of disinfectants. Most Jewish women kept clean houses.

Very often you watched the tragedy of seeing one of the tenants evicted, with their personal belongings in the street. It was caused either by illness or lack of work and inability to raise the rent charged by the landlord. The neighbors would try to contribute funds. The charity societies did a lot of checking before they would offer to help and this embarrassed and hurt the evicted family.

There was a lot of hunger, usually the result of a prolonged strike in the garment industry in which most of the tenants were employed. The union was not strong enough in those days to help financially a sick tenant. Child labor was not uncommon. The workers would take work home to add to their small income and worked all hours of the night in their apartments. These shops were considered sweat-shops and the unions condemned this practice.

The work week started on Monday and Orthodox families stopped working on Friday at sundown. Sabbath was strictly observed on the East Side and most stores were closed until Sunday morning. The men and women went to the synagogue during the day and prayed. The Orthodox synagogue had a balcony which separated the women from the men while praying. There was usually a curtain which prevented the men from being disturbed from their prayers by the presence of the women in the synagogue. I visited the homes of my friends whose parents were Orthodox and observed their customs. They sang songs in praise of the Lord and really had a day of rest. The women prepared a meal called *shulent* [*sic — cholent*, a Sabbath stew] which was baked in the neighborhood oven and then kept warm in their own ovens. There was no smoking or carrying money on one's person and no one used the street transportation on shabbos; everyone walked and paraded their shabbos clothes.

I recall that there were horse drawn cars on Delancey Street and Houston Street and that in the bad snow storms the horses would slip on the ice and had to be assisted to their feet by the passengers getting together. If someone from uptown came to the East Side in their Ford and stalled, the populace would yell, "Get a horse!"

Since the holidays took place in the spring and the fall, my father would take the family out to get new clothes for the year. We were always growing out of our shoes. We all welcomed hand me downs if they were in good condition from our families, like coats and pants. Shoes were never available as they were worn through before the holiday season.

My father's brother was single and handsome and when he came to New York City he lived in our house until he was introduced to a very lovely young lady whom he married. Since he was not married and could save his money, he was able to accumulate enough capital to go into the umbrella handle manufacturing business. My father worked for him from that time until his death at the age of 78 on April 6, 1948. He was the foreman and merely earned a living. My uncle became a rich man because he was able to invest his surplus earnings in real estate. When he married he lived in Brooklyn and had hot water, a bathroom and other luxuries not usually possessed by the immigrants. He even purchased a piano on which his daughter received piano lessons from a private tutor. I visited their home many times and acted as a baby sitter for my uncle's children. For this service I received a family dinner and a piece of cake.

My father worked seven days a week and in the evenings would carry the heavy wine press on his back up four and five flights of stairs for women who wanted wine pressed from grapes purchased from upper New York State or California. He received nominal compensation, but this was a help to him to support his family. The women liked him because he was cheerful and friendly and, since he read the daily papers, kept them abreast of the news of the world. They confided in him because he made excellent wine and did not cheat them.

Besides being the foreman and in charge of the factory output, my father ran a saw cutting machine. He had an accident and cut off almost half a finger but never complained about this. There was no compensation insurance in those years.

The children in the tenements attended the public school across the street from the building. We watched for the opening of the school gates and scrambled down the three floors to the school in order not to be late. We attended this school from the kindergarten until the sixth grade and then were transferred to another school until we reached the eighth grade and were graduated from public school with an elementary school diploma. I still remember a Miss Hoburg, a strict disciplinarian who really taught the three R's. We were all afraid of her but realized what a good teacher she was. When you were promoted from her class, you could do arithmetic, write a legible handwriting and spell accurately. I remember the many spelling bees in which competition was very keen. The students obeyed without retort. The relationship was not personal and she used the ruler frequently over our knuckles.

The school day would start with the general assembly at which excerpts from the Bible were read and beautiful hymns were sung. The Pledge of Allegiance to the Flag of the United States was also recited.

If we were fourteen years of age when we graduated from elementary school, we applied for working papers and went to work in the factories in order to earn some money for the family. However, those who were under fourteen had to go to high school. I walked to Washington Irving High School, which was about two miles each way in rain, snow or sunshine. I attended a commercial course which prepared me for either bookkeeping or stenographic employment. Some parents sent their children to high school to take an academic course to prepare them for such professions as teachers, lawyers, doctors or musicians. Some children attended the school to prepare for the stage or ballet. All the parents were eager that their children have an education and were willing to sacrifice for the cost. I attended Washington Irving School during World War I and remember the Preparedness Parade that we participated in. We had a great many Liberty Bond sales and entertainers who encouraged purchases of bonds. When the war was over, the armistice was signed, and the League of Nations thought to be the solution to the world's problems, we were all happy.

We all waited for Papa to come home from work before we sat down to eat supper, which consisted of soup, bread, boiled beef and some fruit. We all waited to see what goodies Papa would produce from the brown bags.

I recall the children having boils, the whooping cough and diphtheria and bronchial colds and my mother taking them to the free clinic on

Essex Street.

My mother had always had trouble with her ears even when she was in Europe but simply ignored the pain. When I was eight years of age, after a period of great pain she agreed to go to the Eye and Ear Hospital for treatment. However, she worried too much about the children and decided not to stay. By this time she had borne six children but two died in infancy. The children were aged one to twelve, three girls and a boy. She worshipped my brother Willie and had made great plans for his bar mitzvah. She purchased a sewing machine on time payments and with the aid of her neighbors learned to operate it and make dresses for the children and herself. She hired a rabbi to help my brother prepare for his bar mitzvah and was very happy anticipating the big event. However, this was not to be. She suddenly had a bad attack of her ears and had to be rushed for an emergency mastoid operation to a private Jewish hospital, which was not equipped to handle mastoid cases, and so she died. I can remember her telling me to watch the two younger children and not let them go to the front windows looking into the street and not to fight with my older brother who picked on me.

She never came back, except that the funeral took place from our apartment and we children were not allowed to look at her face. I remember walking with my two sisters holding their hands, behind the hearse on the street on the way to the synagogue where kaddish was recited by my father. My brother was thirteen on June 30th and so was bar mitzvahed without any special party. He, too, said the kaddish. The event of my mother's death affected me so that I began to tremble in school and my teachers wrote notes requesting that I be taken to the doctor for treatment. I did go to the lodge doctor but he could do nothing for me. I eventually recovered on my own after a session with black magic.

My father tried to take care of the children himself for several months and even took the pre-school children to a nursery. They cried when he left them. He arranged with the grocer to give me crackers and milk when I came from school. It became too difficult for him to handle the house and the children and so he decided to marry a widow who had no children of her own and had been employed as a housekeeper for hire. He was introduced to her by a matchmaker. She appeared to be a strong woman, but it turned out that she was ill with a disease which the doctors could not diagnose. It was a sort of hiccup with loud bark-like echoes. At first we children were frightened but after a time we learned to live with it. She was a Galician from the country of Austria and my father teased her by saying that she never wore shoes in Europe. She responded that it was true but that she was healthy and had rosy cheeks and did wear shoes on the Sabbath. She was an uneducated woman with no understanding regarding the raising of children and so we practically raised ourselves. Because she pulled my hair, I refused to let her wash and comb my long curls. Consequently I caught lice and was sent home from school to be treated by a woman who specialized in delousing afflicted school children.

My aunt Esther, whom I loved very dearly and who was my father's best friend and confidant, consented to wash my hair and to curl it and make me pretty. I recall that she always gave me a fresh egg shampoo. My father in turn helped his sister with the fruit stand so that she could take care of her house chores and her own five children. My aunt was an excellent cook and every Friday made the most delicious apple strudel which she gave me for the children and myself.

On Saturday the parents got rid of the children by sending them to the movies. The price was two children for a nickel and we would stand around the movies waiting for someone to offer their three pennies. We usually packed a lunch and watched the showing of the movie over and over again and did not leave until our parents forcibly took us out screaming. Very often the movie would break down but this did not bother us any. This was just an excuse to throw things at each other. The movie operator always had someone with some perfume to fumigate the premises, which became very smelly after a while. We children loved the cowboy and Indian movies, the Charlie Chaplin and the continuous movies where the heroine was always saved in the nick of time, like the Pearl White series.

When I learned about the public library I acquired a card allowing me to withdraw several books to read at my leisure at home. I usually went to the library after getting out of school at 3:00 o'clock in the afternoon and stayed until around supper time. Because the library was heated in the fall and winter, I usually did my homework there until the librarian asked us to leave because there was too much noise.

I also learned about the reading room in the Educational Alliance which was warm and quiet and where a dictionary was available, and so on Sundays I went there, even though it was about ten blocks away. We had no money for transportation and usually walked the distance in fair or bad weather.

I recall that the streets were dirty and cluttered with garbage and debris. I can distinctly remember garbage bags descending into the street from the tenement apartment and that you were lucky not to be hit. This was because people were scared to go into the cellar with their garbage or were too lazy to take the garbage out during the day.

Life was not easy and every neighbor knew the other neighbor's troubles and joys. One did not move often and so life-long friendships were cultivated. We all came from different backgrounds. My parents were of Rumanian extraction. I had several friends whose parents were Polish, Russian, German, Austrian and English. Most of the neighbors worked with their hands and raised their families with the hope that their children would learn professions and better themselves. They were in touch with their families and encouraged immigration to the United States so that they would not be alone.

As children of immigrants, we were anxious to learn from the people who were Americanized and who had acquired a degree of success since their arrival. Thus we discovered the various settlement houses maintained on the East Side by the ultra-rich uptown Jews. There was the Eldridge Street Settlement, the Grand Street Settlement and the Recreation Rooms and Settlement which was located on Chrystie Street and which my friends and I attended. I remember meeting Mrs. Franklin D. Roosevelt and other social workers at the settlement. The workers encouraged education and established small grants for worthy students. We formed social and educational clubs and had a counselor to advise and direct our activities. We had a gymnasium where we played basketball and danced. We were in a fine environment and off the streets. We were given tickets to the theatre, concerts, opera, ballet and lectures free of charge and we had a free nursing service.

In the summertime we attended the camps maintained by the State in the Bear Mountain district and learned to swim, hike and love and appreciate nature. We also took trains which ran directly to the various beaches. Coney Island was a favorite of the East Side residents because of its proximity. We usually wore our bathing suits under our outer clothes.

New York City was run by politicians and Tammany Hall was in full sway. They appeared to help the very poor by giving them coal and food, but this was not a solution to the terrible curse of poverty of the East Side. President Woodrow Wilson was elected President of the United States [in 1913] and the populace expected great things from the new administration.

In the house next to ours on the same street lived a known prostitute, who was known as Mollie the *bumiker*. The police apparently did not concern themselves about Mollie but we girls were aware of the situation and steered clear of her.

Crime was rampant but nothing serious was ever done to completely stop it. We were grateful if none of our family became involved. My younger sister once was present when a murder was committed before her very eyes by a gangster in front of my Aunt Esther's pushcart. She told my aunt that she could identify the man, but my aunt placed her hand on her mouth and told her not to speak or say anything because if she did they would kill her. She immediately sent her upstairs so that she would not say anything to the police who arrived and made inquiries.

The man who managed the tenement house where we lived collected the rents for the landlord and was a small politician associated with Tammany Hall. He had a fire and life insurance agency in his apartment from which he made a fair living. He was able to obtain votes during elections in return for small favors to the voters. He was also a bondman who was able to have the criminals released on bail while awaiting trial. Gangs were common and many gang wars were engaged in causing death to innocent bystanders. There were many men and women who were socialists and condemned the practices of Tammany Hall. I knew personally that the votes were fraudulent but as the saying went, "Who could fight city hall?"

The tenements were infested and the only way out was when the children went to work and added their earnings to the family income, and so families started to move to the Bronx, Brooklyn and Long Island. For a time it seemed as though we were having some form of prosperity. The native-born population quickly assimilated and became part and parcel of a new generation looking for a better future for their children.

I remember several neighbors in the tenement. One was a cantor who had a son who graduated as a pharmacist. One neighbor was an actress who performed on the Jewish stage. The Yiddish stage was very popular with the immigrants and they had many popular stars. Many actresses and actors after learning English became popular on the American stage.

A dear friend of mine whose parents were first cousins were very Orthodox in their practice of the religion. She became mentally and emotionally ill and was sent to several mental institutions. She eventually married but had many spells of mental illness. At the present time she is in a mental institution with no hope of recovery. One of my personal friends became a ballet dancer and eventually a social worker and became the headworker for the Educational Alliance. Another friend obtained a scholarship and was graduated from Cornell University as a doctor and psychiatrist. She was a fine violinist. Her father was a tailor and loved music. Still another friend, who attended high school with me at night, became a famous sculptor. He studied in Europe and America and obtained many scholarships and eventually was knighted by the English queen.

The father of one of the families next door on the third floor was a consumptive and his wife helped him sell merchandise on the pushcart. His wife became sick with cancer and died soon thereafter. His death followed shortly and there were three children left orphans. One of the children was adopted because she was very pretty, and the other two children were helped by neighbors and friends until some relatives appeared and took charge of them.

There were many weddings and my father was usually invited as he was the life of the party and outdanced all the guests. The weddings lasted until dawn. Everyone loved my father because he was kind, compassionate and understood the needs and plight of his friends.

While we were still living on the East Side, my very best friend Pauline and I decided to take an academic course at the East Side Evening High School for Men. We were both A students and apparently interested the man in charge of admitting students. Pauline's mother disapproved of Pauline's going to school at night with only boys and so she was forced to drop out. I considered this an opportunity to prove that girls were as bright as boys. I continued going to school and eventually graduated with an academic diploma. I was secretary of the school and treasurer of my graduating class. I was also the hiking director for our walks on Sunday mornings. I was very popular in the school and after my graduation the school became a co-educational high school.

I qualified to attend law school at New York University and eventually received both the degrees of L.L.B and L.L.M. from New York University. I was so busy studying law that I had no time for romance and had very few boyfriends. I was inspired to study law because I had had a part time job with a woman criminal attorney and I had dreams of helping my fellow man in an ailing world to acquire justice and peace. The first legal work I had was as a law clerk with the munificent salary of $5.00 a week. I could not afford to work for such a small salary and so quit the job and was out of work.

The Depression hit New York City sooner than many other cities and so when I found myself out of work I listened to my brother's suggestion that I come to Los Angeles where there were many opportunities. I left my father and stepmother who had raised me and went to Los Angeles to start a new adventure in living. She died soon thereafter from a heart attack and my father remarried a younger widow who had a son living with her. He continued working for his brother and kept asking me to return home. I did not want to admit defeat and so stayed on, struggling to make a living wage. I wrote glowing letters to my father, but he seemed to see through them. He knew that I was unhappy and sent me a check to come home, but I immediately returned it to him and told him that I would manage somehow. I loved my father very much and only have the dearest and kindest memories and loving thoughts of him as a father to this very day.

Each morning was a challenge that God would provide for a better day.

_____

*The daughter of Jewish immigrants from Rumania,
Ida Rothman Feely herself was American-born. She had studied law
at New York University, yet, although she earned various
law degrees, life was hard on New York's Lower East Side, and when the
Depression made it particularly difficult to earn a decent living in
New York, Mrs. Feely moved to Los Angeles for a new start.*

Crowded Districts

Lillian Wald

𝕵 n bringing a report of the crowded districts of great cities to you today, I am aware that whatever I could say to impress you would be from the personal experiences and conclusions obtained by some years' residence in such a quarter of one city only, or the less valuable observations made as visitor and stranger to like districts in other cities. But before we enter into particular descriptions or the ethics of their existence anywhere, I would remind you of the real insight that may be obtained by all, not only of the congested regions of great cities but of the causes and results of their existence.

Such important education is to be found in the clear reading of official reports, vital statistics, labor reports and annuals, tenement-house reports, police records, school reports, charity organizations and institution year-books — such literature as may be had for the asking, yet is, in many ways, the important social, history-making literature of our times. Then, more interesting, perhaps, are the evidences that may be found in stories and magazine articles, by the residents of social settlements and missions, the thoughts of visiting philosophers, who, eager to know the crowds, have camped for a time in these backyards of our great cities, and have given the fruit of their meditations to others. There are the deeper works of students of sociology, who have looked upon these crowded districts as human laboratories, coldly, or inspired by a higher than scientific interest, a human one, to know the people, the men and the women, the children and the conditions that make "masses" and "districts" and "East Sides," have brought their experiences to scholarly consideration. Knowing that these things are, they must next see why, and perhaps have thus furnished what has been likened to the ophthalmoscope, the instrument that made it possible to see into the eye, and thus revealing the disease, gave the physician the opportunity of curing it. Furnished with such an ophthalmoscope, the physician of social wrongs may heal and take from modern civilization its most baneful growth.

Such reading as this suggests might be called "dry," mere skeletons of figures to be recognized only by people "interested in that sort of thing," literature not to be found in any but the specialist's library. But it is not dry; and even if so, it is a literature that concerns us all, more than any news compiled, and if awaiting readers now, will some day *force* the attention of the whole world. But read each figure a human being: read that every wretched unlighted tenement described is a *home* for people, men and women, old and young, with the strength and the weaknesses, the good and the bad, the appetites and wants common to all. Read, in descriptions of sweatshops, factories, and long-hour workdays, the difficulty, the impossibility of well-ordered living under the conditions outlined. Understanding reading of these things must bring a sense of fairness outraged, the disquieting conviction that something is wrong somewhere, and turning to your own contrasting life, you will feel a responsibility of the *how* and the *why* and the *wherefore.* Say to yourself, "If there is a wrong in our midst, what can *I* do? What is *my* responsibility? Who is to blame? Do *I* owe reparation?"

All of this is a plea for the intelligent reading of the things that pertain to the people of the crowded districts of all cities, that something more may be given to the subject than the few moments in a convention's program; that the suggestion may be made, and the thought carried home that more carefully-prepared witnesses are yours to be called up at all times and for the asking.

Agreeing that a common condition must be produced by a common cause, in order to understand its life anywhere, we need only confine ourselves to a study of the crowded district that is familiar to the witness you have called up today. As it is a crowded district of our [New York] metropolis, it belongs to all the country, and therefore is yours. It presents, only in a greater degree due to an unfortunate geographical condition, the state of people anywhere who are poor, and unlearned, and clannish, and strange. Though a sweeping classification is an easy way of tabulating, it is unjust to say of our neighbors, the greater number of whom are Russian or Polish Jews, that they are the least clean, the most unlovely and ungrateful, and terms put more harshly. This is a generalization to be denied, excepting to put out that an equal degree of ignorance and an equal depth of poverty will create the same conditions of filth and unattractiveness, whether found among Russians, Italians, or Irish. It is more often a cause of astonishment to us to find polished brass and scrubbed floors under difficult circumstances than to find inexcusable uncleanliness; and the lessons of patience and affection and courtesy are constantly presented to us by them.

Let us take for definite allusion three wards of New York, those in my immediate neighborhood, the seventh, tenth, and eleventh, populated, according to the last census, by 190,388 people, covering 504 acres—something over 377 people to each acre—including in these figures, however, one division of thirty-two acres—Second, Columbia, Rivington, and Clinton Streets (between Avenues B and D south of Second Street)—with 986.4 persons to every acre of the thirty-two, representing the most crowded community on the face of the earth.

Now, I do not know what these figures may bring up to your vision; to one who has seen the portion of the city referred to, in summer and winter, by day and by night, they bring up a dark picture of this small part of an English-speaking city, peopled by nearly 200,000, the greater number of whom speak an unknown tongue; foreigners with foreign standards of living, often having been forced to leave their homes; coming here with the inheritances of mistrust and a low standard of living; coming, though, with high hopes of a new start, in a country where education is possible to all, where the poorest may be respected, and where democracy sways; coming here likewise with lower aspirations, or no aspiration at all; brought here in the expectation of profiting by the wealth and generosity of the country, without a thought of contributing to it. These parasites are a small number in the very large tenement-house population of New York, which is eight-fifteenths of the whole.

If to dwell upon the newly arrived would divert our discussion to that of the restriction of emigration, let us rather consider what those who are here already actually experience: what opportunities the children of the poorly paid and unskilled workers have; what effect it may have upon the circulation of the body politic, to infuse into its arteries the life-current of people who live day after day under conditions disadvantageous to growth, civic, physical, and moral.

The crowding you may realize; the language of the street is a jargon; the signs over the places of business are frequently in Hebrew with misspelled English translations, occasionally furnishing grim humor to the foreigner, for here *you* are the foreigner yourself, in your own home. Your eye is met by such business notices as: "Marriages legally performed inside," and competitor offers to perform the same service cheaper than anyone else, and in most approved style; and by the hand-organ, with or without a monkey — the greatest delight of the street — and the prettiest dancing of the prettiest, most neglected looking children that can be seen anywhere. The houses are dilapidated, filth-infected, and dark; old houses, once the homes of the wealthy and fastidious, converted to present uses by a process of decay, and maintained at the smallest expense possible to bring the largest returns possible; rear tenements, built upon what was left of the city lots of front houses; houses facing the street, utilizing the space that was once a garden; tall new tenements built upon single city lots 25 x 100 feet, with four families to a floor, each single lot tenanted by twenty to twenty-four different families; with saloon and one store generally in the basement. This variety of tenement-house, the familiar "double-decker," occupying 86 to 90 percent of the lot's depth, is in many ways worse than the old remodeled residence, its air-shafts and basement furnishing contaminated air and frequent fires to its one hundred to one hundred and fifty inhabitants. The houses are not fireproof, though provided with fire-escapes; and the almost constant use of kerosene, the darkness, the many children, the occupations in the houses, are causes of frequent fires. The Fire Department records show that in this third of the population of New York, the fires are more than one-half the whole number, and deaths and accidents are very frequent.

There are two so-called "model tenements" in the region we are describing, and in one part of this area, several houses occupied by single families, and at least two streets wide and favorably situated; but there are blocks almost entirely covered by buildings, one (brought up before the Tenement-Houses Commission of 1894) covering 93 percent of the total area, and a total area of thirty-four blocks showing 78 percent built upon.

The very small space between the houses, sometimes only 18 inches, is utilized for the drying of clothes and as a receptacle for refuse of all

Lillian Wald

kinds. The narrow street-space is a jostling, shoving, pushcart market for the selling of over-ripe fruit, fish, vegetables, etc. The halls of the houses are so dark that groping is the method of movement in them, and the little girl described hers when she lost something and said:"Oh! I'll find it at night when the gas is lighted." The nurses never overcome the fear of trampling on the children in the hall or on the street, a sound warning them when to tread carefully, or sometimes out of the darkness a tiny hand on the railing shocking suddenly with the sense of accident averted. It is not uncommon to go in daytime into the closet-room with candle in hand, in order to be able to see the patient at all; nor is it uncommon to go at night and see ten or eleven people occupying two small rooms — people who have been working all day, freed for the night's rest, stretched on the floor, one next to the other, dividing the pillows, different sexes, not always the same family, for there are "boarders," who pay a small sum for shelter, among their own, the family glad of the help toward paying the rent. The price of rooms in the most wretched basement in the rear tenements is so high in comparison with the wage earned that it is for those who have employment based on something like regular income about one-fourth of the whole. But it must be remembered that few trades give employment all the year round. We hear more often than any other plaint that of the uncertainty of having a roof; the failure comes so often, and with it the "dispossess paper," that the sight of the house-hold effects on the sidewalk following its presentment is too common to collect a crowd, where crowds collect quickly.

During the hot months of July and August is the time to observe a crowded district at its worst. The vermin and the heat drive the people to the streets, which are crowded with these unfortunates the greater part of the night. Mothers sit on the curbstone with nursing babies, and the cool of the door-stone is coveted for a pillow, or, the refreshment of sleep on the roof or in the courts between the houses is sought, unless, indeed, the odors of the closets there are worse than the vermin or the heat within.

On the other hand, within these tenements are sometimes found the most scrupulously kept rooms; plants by the windows, happiness, and a real home; courtesy, devotion, and charity, such as one may seek for among the elect of the earth, and reverence; sufficient evidence of the original nobility of character, which can remain high despite all discouragements.

But the more frequent picture is that of the overcrowded rooms, denying the privacy and sacredness of homelife. Outside the house there is almost no park or playground for the children — nothing but the sidewalks and streets. Games for the boys are of necessity reduced to "leap-frog," "craps," or tossing pennies.

School-time comes, and the population increases so rapidly that, with the best intentions, it seems impossible to provide place, and with a less keen sense of responsibility, the worst occurs. An unlettered, indifferent parent, exhorted and then informed that education is compulsory, finally does exert himself to claim the place for his children in the school, to learn that compulsory education acts and truant officers are superfluous matters, since there is no place in the school for his children. There is considerable discrepancy in the figures giving the number of children out of school at present — 400 in one school alone of the region I am making special reference to today.

The law says that the child must be in school until fourteen, that he or she may not be employed under that age; and as nothing more than the parent's testimony is required to give the child to the [sweat] shops, the temptation to perjury is apparent.

We come now to the sweatshops, labor in which is the principal occupation of our neighbors. Where a "union" has been established and is strong, the workday may be ten hours; where the trade is unorganized (and that is more likely to be among unskilled, therefore the poor, therefore the least educated) the workday is more often fourteen hours. Have you heard of the diseases most prevalent among people who work in contaminated air, and then go home to sleep under the same conditions? In the Nurses' Settlement [established in 1895 on Henry Street] consumption is spoken of as "tailors' disease."

Have you watched the drive, drive, drive of men and women at the machines, over cigar or cigarette making? Have you peeped down into the cellars, and seen the rags sorted, the shirts made, the washing done, shoes cobbled, cheese and bread made? Have you watched the making of the collars, passementerie [trimming], clothing, cloaks, and artificial flowers, the curling of feathers, the steaming of hats, the manufacture of neckties and boxes, the production of the whole long list of necessaries and luxuries for other people? Have you watched where the workers were laboring under the indifference or absenteeism of the employer — working, working, working, until the pain in watching the ceaseless strain becomes unendurable, and you cry out against the inhumanity of it all? Cry out because you can see how impossible it is for these men and women to have the leisure or the strength to rear their children into stalwart men and women, into citizens with intelligent reasoning of how to govern themselves or to choose their governors.

I bring up again for the thousandth time in excuse for uncleanliness or a low standard of social or moral ethics, when such exist, no education, crowded, dark rooms for a home, no time or opportunities for proper cleanliness, no opportunities for healthful pleasures; grinding work and small pay; no work, and then the necessaries of life a gift. "Charity covers a multitude of sins," but does not wipe them out. Anxiety lest ends might not meet excludes even conversation in the home. All negatives are shifts to make ends meet; laws are evaded, breeding contempt for law and order. Finally, there is the dumb discontent provoked into loud resentment; the distrust of class, creating leaders of their own who know what they have not, who can comprehend what they want. There can be no denial that the poor are poorer, that what is called "class feeling" has been intensified. This last election [William McKinley for the Republicans emerging the victor over William Jennings Bryan for the Democrats and John Palmer for the "gold Democrats"] made many people see for the first time there was what one side called revolt, that a "campaign of education" seemed necessary to save our institutions.

I am fully conscious of not bringing to you a complete picture of even the small section of one city; there is too much to be said. Many dark pictures have been omitted. There has been no reference to the peddlers who have no trade, only the instinct of trade, many of whom, however, are skilled workmen with no demand for their skill, obliged in dull seasons to do *anything,* and that means a basket, a box, or a pushcart, with some small outlay for stock; not that the occupation is desirable but because that is all that is left, and work in the busy season has not paid enough to carry the family over.

Also should I like to dwell upon the affection and sobriety of our neighbors; the gratitude for courtesies, and the response to efforts for education among the children; the honest return of money loaned to them; the eagerness to show their patriotism, as instanced when the Russian brought his violin to us to show how well he had learned "our" national air, and forthwith played "After the ball is over" — he had come here three years ago, when that seemed the song of America — and the pride in having attained citizenship, when they do, framing and hanging the official testimony on the wall, though the vaccination certificate has been thus honored also.

I would not be reporting the crowded district of any city unless the many philanthropic efforts for relief of actual physical suffering were brought up. So numerous are these efforts in this city that it would appear as if no thought or plan of charity had been omitted, until the wise administration of charity and the study of the people who prefer to receive gratuitously instead of to work, has become a profession. We see from our East Side point of view the charities in operation, and their results, good or bad — good, if they are educational in any way (but this is a subject distinct in itself). You have not more than a suggestion of the features of life in a neighborhood. This avails nothing, however, if you do not seek for confirmation and elaboration of these suggestions; realize with me that a crowded district in its entirety is too great for single handling, too serious for dismissal in an afternoon paper.

I might appeal to your self-interests to recognize the close relationships between the crowded districts of great cities and the more fortunate regions; might prove that the danger of infected and unsanitary tenements are your direct affairs; tell of the things made in rooms where infectious diseases were or had been; — evidences of the dying consumptive working at cigarettes; of the filthy basement where the sick girl lay, and where candy was being made; of the felt slippers sewed in the room where scarlet fever and diphtheria were; or of the servant girl coming home to visit in similar circumstances and returning to the baby.

There is a higher, juster appeal that your sense of responsibility will make to you. If the homes are poor, build others; not as charities, but as investments, satisifed with 4 percent return, in planning which have the comfort and education of the tenants in view. The testimony of people here and elsewhere who have had practical experience, proves that such investments pay in every way, and that almost all have given a satisfactory return upon the investment of money. Time and education, both of which are slow, are required to alter many things; but you can begin it for others and yourselves. You can help the labor difficulty by comprehending what a fair condition of labor is. If you have no [mutual aid] "consumers' league" to receive your pledge, pledge its principles to yourself. If there is a strike, try to discover both sides of the question, not only the one vulgarly holding your butter, but the other's grievance also; not rejoicing in the workingman's failure without understanding (if that is possible) what was behind the discontent. Be fair enough to help that workingman in his way, if you can see that his way is right. Listen to the cries that come from crowded districts. Their people are patient, and are not demanding overmuch. The respectable workingman, the father of the children, is wanting work, and when he does work, sufficient pay for it, to be sure of a roof and life-sustaining food and some leisure, to know a world that is not only working and eating and sleeping. Don't you see how the lack of that must bring the begging letter, at first the shamefaced appeal for help that has not been earned, and then the indifference, and then the going-down and all the things debasing to manhood? It is *work* and *sufficient pay* for it that is the just demand. Last week a woman asked for some aid, and a few days later wrote that she would not require any, as God has sent her husband two days' work.

Do all that you can to make public sentiment for fair play in work and play. Carry the thought of the workers with you when you are shopping. If the cry from the crowded district is good for food, you will give that; but in relieving, give wisely and adequately, and see if the cause of that cry can be removed.

Last of all, you would be helping the labor and the unemployed question by making domestic service desirable, recognizing the need here also of stated hours, freedom, and occasional privacy. There is often as great a distance between drawing-room and kitchen as between uptown and downtown.

Let me retire as witness now and ending, bring Phillips Brooks' voice back to you for inspiration and right understanding of our mutual obligations: "The universal blunder of this world is in thinking that there are certain persons put into the world to govern, and certain others to obey. Everybody is in this world to govern, and everybody to obey. Men are coming to see that beyond and above this individualism there is something higher — Mutualism. Don't you see that in this Mutualism the world becomes an entirely different thing? Men's dreams are after the perfect world of Mutualism; men will think of it in the midst of the deepest subjection to the false conditions under which they are now living. This is new life, where service is universal law."

———

*Dissension between Jews of Central European
antecedents and the East European newcomers was common in
turn-of-the-century America. But there were always
men and women who disregarded ethnic and class prejudice and made
it their life's work to help the immigrant to overcome
the wretchedness of the tenement scene. One of them was Lillian
Wald (1867-1940), a far-sighted social worker,
founder of the famous Henry Street settlement, who,
aware of the "nobility of character"
she sensed emerging from New York's Lower East Side,
took up the cause of the immigrant.
At New York, in mid-November of 1896, she presented her views
to Jewish women of "uptown" Central European stock
at the first convention of the
National Council of Jewish Women, a group founded
three years earlier, largely as a
philanthropic effort on behalf of immigrants.*

———

*Jewish immigrants arriving at the North German Lloyd wharf
in Galveston, Texas (Courtesy of Institute of Texan Cultures)*

The Grateful Thread

Jeannette W. Bernstein

M erchant, scholar, musician, teacher, public relations, builder, soldier and sailor, these were the diversified contributions to their beloved country of Harry Warshavsky and his wife, Lizzie. Average Americans, they represent the drab little thread in the brilliant tapestry that is the United States of America.

Within each of us there lies an unwritten book, the story of one's life that surely is different from all other lives. Everyone is not endowed with a facile pen nor with the skill to embellish with description and dramatic force, to expand a tale of one little family into a story that will merit publication. Yet I feel that the lives of my parents portray such a definite period in the development of America that it should be recorded.

America, to me, has always appeared as a gigantic tapestry. Some of her founders and illustrious citizens are the colorful threads that produced the pictures and patterns that people notice and admire and praise. But many, many more of the threads were the drab hue of the background material through which the colors were drawn.

Such a thread was Harry Jacob Warshavsky who came to America in the 1880's. He never did anything great nor became rich, but he was perhaps most typical of the great mass of Russian Jews who came to America with hopes and dreams, who had been told the streets of New York were paved with gold. What many of them found instead was crowded ghettos, exploitation of labor in sweat shops. Yet they felt themselves extremely fortunate to be in America where each preceding immigrant held out a helping hand to the new one.

My father was a Hebrew scholar in Russia, no doubt a yeshiva student, but he used to tell of his desire to read other books than biblical ones. I recall his story of having gone through all the "learning," through the Torah [Pentateuch] and Gemorrah [Talmud], even having read Cabala [the mystic books of early Jewry]. Yet he would sneak into a Russian cobbler's shop to learn to read the Russian language so other channels could be opened to him. His nephew tells me Papa was only thirteen when he was summoned before a group of rabbis and scolded and quizzed because he dared to read Russian novels and history. He answered his test so well that his uncle, who reared the orphaned Harry, gave his consent to outside reading.

To speak to a Russian, much less use the Russian tongue, was taboo for pious Jews. They had been driven to hatred and fear of the aristocrats, the officers, and the Cossacks because of pogroms. Too often the Cossacks came flying through the village on their speeding horses, flaying their whips and burning the houses, then rushing on. In fact, it was because of the pogroms of the eighties that the great wave of immigrants flooded into America.

The court and the army were the aristocrats — the Cossacks, the men with the whips; the peasants, the serfs, and the Jews the scapegoats, the victims. No wonder no patriotic allegiance to the native land could be felt by the young conscriptees. At twenty-one came the call to the army of Czar Nicholas II. This took Harry into the barracks town of Szaslav in the Ukraine. Here he met my mother. But that comes later. One night he and his soldier friend returned to the barracks a few minutes late. Papa saw a Russian officer beat his companion to death with a leather whip. He knew then he could be next. So he quietly went about the business of planning an escape from the army to which he felt no loyalty. He slipped across the Russian border in a load of hay and boarded a boat to America. He was grateful even for his passage in the steerage of the Hamburg Line, where the people were packed into the hold like sardines, sleeping in many small berths — as many as the space could accommodate.

At Castle Garden, because he could not pronounce his name to suit those in charge, the name of Warshavsky was slapped onto him. I've often thought that maybe there are so many unrelated Warshavskys in America for the same reason. A brother who came to Chicago later accepted that name so he could carry the same one as Papa.

———

Harry Jacob arrived in St. Louis, Missouri, in the late 1880's with a dollar and a half in cash and the name of one friend. This fact seems worth recording. No immigrant of today could have this opportunity, nor be allowed to enter this country with a dollar and a half in cash and that nebulous thing — a friend. In those days a friend came forward despite his own limited resources. Papa had taught Hebrew to the sons of Max Madansky in Russia; that was the needle that held the tiny thread that this relationship wove into the tapestry of America.

The friend equipped Papa with a small peddler's pack. As I recall his tale, it was more of a door to door satchel of threads and small wares. Many are the funny stories of the encounters of the non-English-speaking canvasser such as the one about the peddler friend Nottie who said, "How do they all know my name? They say to me right away, 'Nottie Gay' (not today). So I gay." *Gay* means go in Yiddish.

Well Harry the scholar didn't do well as a door to door salesman, so he became a presser in a pants factory. He had no real trade except teaching. In one year he saved up enough to send transportation money to the girl he remembered in the barracks town of Szaslav.

I record the following because I think it symbolic of the era and the yearning to get out of Czarist Russia. Miriam Elizabeth Shapiro finally consented to come to St. Louis and marry Harry. Imagine her amazement when she found her suitor was the short serious man, not his tall handsome companion (the one whom the officer had beaten to death). She was here, Papa was persuasive and so they were married in the house of the friend who had given mother her temporary home. Lizzie, as Papa called her, was a beautiful, petite, curly-haired brunette with a sparkling personality. No wonder the quiet Harry carried her in his heart until she married him and forever after.

Mama was pert, aggressive, a born saleswoman who took the initiative throughout their long marriage. Her business aptitude was developed in Russia where she attended the shop of her father, Joseph Shapiro, the silversmith. Grandfather must have been an able craftsman for he made handwrought table services for the officers of the barracks. One nephew apprenticed to him became a most skilled platinum smith here in America. We still wear the graceful jewelry her cousin designed for my mother in her later years.

Mama and Papa were established in their own apartment. They took in a boarder to supplement their income and settled down to the business of living. First came my sister Annie, then Sarah, then a brother who succumbed soon after his birth. I didn't enter the picture until 1898. The pressure of housework and rapidly arriving babies made my mother very melancholy. She tells of going into the children's room and looking at two heads and four feet and saying, "Can these be mine?" I'm sure she missed the carefree gaiety of her life in her father's shop, her camaraderie with her father and brother whom she adored, maybe the pear trees in the yard of her home — I recall she spoke of those pear trees often. But children demand care, and that helped her to come out of her depression.

Then Papa became nearly blind. The intense reading of his early years, and the constant steam from the pressing machine aggravated an eye infection which made it necessary for him to go to a great specialist in New York. And here is where Mama came to life. She arranged for care of the children. In fact, she had brought to America her sister Annie, and Auntie took over the reins of the house while Mama said, "Enough of this nonsense, I'll open a store."

This best demonstrates the spunk of the woman. She had saved one hundred and fifty dollars somehow. She rented a small store near the Union station on Market Street in St. Louis. Mama went into a wholesale house and said, "I have one hundred and fifty dollars, an empty store and five mouths to feed. I want three hundred dollars worth of merchandise; two of this, two of that and lots of empty boxes to fill the shelves." And she got it! The next visit she paid the bill, had an extra hundred and fifty in cash and asked for and got six hundred dollars of merchandise. And Lizzie Warshavsky was in business.

I love her story about leaving a leg of underwear hanging out of the empty box to make it appear so full she couldn't keep the lid down.

Those were the days when it was natural to barter and trade. By the time Papa was cured by the doctor in New York, Mama had a store so packed with merchandise, new and old, they decided to venture into newer fields. They had heard of a small but thriving—nay, booming lumber town in Arkansas. The village was so small it was probably a tiny, tiny dot on the map, but it was filled with men and had few stores, and it was men's merchandise that they had on hand. So off to the village Papa went with his packing cases of merchandise. Mother was a boomer by nature. I'm sure she would have dug oil wells and looked for uranium had she been a man.

———

Papa rented the one brick store in the small town and set up shop. I think this was about the year I was born, 1898, and Mama had visions of rearing her three children in less crowded surroundings. One night the entire block caught on fire. The fire started underneath Papa's store (pure arson) and the mob cried, "Throw the Jew in the fire. He started it for insurance money." God was with him that night. He had applied for an insurance policy which was not yet in effect. The agent was present and quelled the mob when he shouted, "Harry doesn't own a cent of insurance, I know." So Papa returned to St. Louis to help Mama accumulate a new stock.

The next move was to Pocahontas, Arkansas, a hilly town in Randolph County, in the foothills of the Ozarks. The town's population was then one thousand souls. The townsite was built on elevated land. A hill gradually sloped up from the river's edge. Black River it was called and many were the pearls found in its depths. The pearl fishers used to bring their finds to Mama, who acted as middleman between them and the itinerant pearl buyers who made the river towns. She used to tell of handling one pearl that found its way to Tiffany's as a center pearl for a fabulous string.

The very name Pocahontas evokes pictures of Indians roaming the area and memories of Captain John Smith. My strongest memory is that it was very cold in the winter. Jack Frost left his etchings on the glass panes through many months. Maybe storm windows would have kept those fancy designs away, but I used to love the pictures my active imagination could produce from the icy patterns. The low log burning stoves, squatty and oblong, kept our houses warm enough for our Saturday night bath in a round galvanized tub that was filled with water heated on the kitchen stove, a wood burning kitchen range with four burners and an oven, all trimmed with shiny nickle plate. I doubt if even the rich had plumbing in a small Arkansas town at the turn of the century. The business section was built around the courthouse square. Many townspeople were devout German Catholics still speaking their native tongue.

Here my memory has recorded much. I leave the realm of hearsay and write of what I personally recall, except for the beginning, for I was a baby of eighteen months when we moved there and eight years old when we moved away.

The folks built up a comfortable business in a general store — outfitters for the entire family and we had in time a white cottage all

The face of the shtetl — an East European village which many
of the Jewish immigrants had called home

our own. Fruit must have been the main crop there, for I can still recall the luscious, juicy apples, the large yellow apples that had a pear taste, and the strawberries that ripened under the late snow in our own yard.

We were proud of our five-room house. It had hardwood floors throughout, something very special in those days. There was a concrete lined cistern on the back porch, also special because it filtered the water somehow and we didn't have to go into the yard to pull up the well water. And we had an early day garbage disposal — on the hoof. Everybody owned a hog for that one purpose. It was a ritual at our house; Papa would come along; the noon whistle would blow; Papa would call, "Here pig, here pig." And up from the back slope would appear the sow to relish her daily bucket of swill. That pig nearly ruined the marriage of my sister. Someone told the groom. "You can't marry that girl. Her father raised pigs." But he, too, knew the story and laughed it off.

We also owned a guitar that Mama played a little; a mandolin that Mama sat on (as she did on so many of Papa's derby hats); an inexpensive violin that nobody could play, and Papa's piccolo that I never saw him play. The town had a German band. We have a picture of Papa and his piccolo but I wonder if he ever played it. Mama took piano lessons all her life and learned to play one piece, "Over the Waves." No wonder she tried to make musicians of her children, she loved music so.

What I remember best about the store was the watchmaker's corner. (He sublet a small space). For some crazy reason he kept a rattlesnake in a screened cage. Once he put the thing around my five-year-old neck. I can still recall the cold clamminess of that snake. I'm sure its fangs had been removed. Another time it slithered out of the cage. The screams of the female customers closed that episode. Either the jeweler or the snake or both left the store.

Many were the nights I was put to sleep on a high stack of pants while the store was kept open until ten o'clock. Then they would awaken me and I'd stumble the half mile home by foot. Who knew of anything but the long walk then? We had to cross the bridge where a man had been hanged by a lynching party and cold shivers would run up my spine. I know this lynching story is true. Papa had acquired such good status in the community he was invited to participate. He claimed a faintness at the sight of blood and was excused.

Our store was opposite the well on the courthouse square. The well was a fancy contraption. You wound a rope about a cylinder to which was attached a metal handle. Mama had just returned from St. Louis, hot and thirsty. My sister and I rushed over to draw her a cool drink. Sarah got tired of turning the handle. I took over. It was too heavy for me; it slipped from my hands, struck Sarah and nearly killed her. Somehow we managed to get back to the store ourselves. My poor sister nearly died from the accident, but God and a good doctor and Mother pulled her through.

As I write this, I realize living in Pocahontas in the early 1900's was pretty primitive, but I know we all had a jolly though busy life. On Saturdays the maid brought a picnic basket of food to the store. There was not time to go home, so eating facilities were set up in a partition in the back of the store. On one such occasion a gray enamel teapot with a graceful long spout had been used for chicken soup. I spotted it and took it off the stove and put it to my mouth. The boiling grease blistered my mucous membranes all the way down. My screams brought Mama on the run. Fortunately Dr. Pringle's drug store was next door. I'll never know what he used, but no serious harm was done.

There was the day our saleslady, Mimmie, challenged Papa to cut off his handle-bar mustache. He did so and claimed his kiss. My sister and I were sad — we had just bought him a new mustache cup.

It was the era of board sidewalks, both in front and back of the store. I recall clomping along trying so hard to imitate the sound of ladies high heels clicking on the boards.

One year the school closed down and my sister and I attended the convent, high up on a hill. We all carried dust pans or sleds. The boys made a chain and pulled the tiny tots up. It was my first year of school, I recall. After school we would sit on our dust pans and slide down. More fun! I also remember the sisters played snow ball with us at recess time. I was so amazed to see nuns play.

Every pre-Christmas the nuns had a bazaar and carnival. I still recall a yellow satin needle case exquisitely embroidered. What I learned in school I don't remember except a lesson in courtesy between religions. I didn't stand with the other children when they repeated the Lord's Prayer. Sister gently asked me to remain after class. She said, "If I visited your synagogue, I'd stand when you did, it's just being polite." I stood thereafter, willingly.

I don't recall my sister Annie. She died in Pocahontas when she was about eleven years old. She jumped rope a hundred times, drank ice water and contracted pneumonia. Mother grieved deeply for Annie. They tell me she was very brilliant.

Mama was always going to market in St. Louis. I'd be dragged along each time. My aunt took care of me in St. Louis while Mama shopped the wholesale houses. I contracted every kind of measles known, a different one each visit. I bet I was a nuisance to my busy mother and certainly to my aunt and Uncle Will. I think I wasn't so welcome after their own son Joe was born.

On one trip a sly conductor visited with me and another little traveler and asked our ages. I had just had a birthday and replied, "I was six years old on the twenty-second of January." Mama had neglected to mention this, so he made her buy a ticket for me. After that, I got left home with Papa and the maid, that is, most of the time.

My sister and I were absolute opposites. She was a brunette and very chubby and healthy. I was almost a platinum blonde and painfully skinny. Sarah was always good in school, bringing home prizes. One, I recall, was *Little Women* by Louisa Mae Alcott. This she won while we still lived in Pocahontas. Another she won was *Black Beauty*. Every girl simply had to own and read these two books.

I was known as puny, a delicate, thin child. One year the folks decided a summer on a farm would fatten me up, so on a farm I went. These things I best recall — tables laden with food, overflowing with jellies and hot breads and cakes and pies, in addition to the substantial meat, potatoes, corn on the cob and other vegetables. I name them in the order of importance to my six years. So I was stuffed like the country goose!

Then there was the day we children walked to the country store, and were chased by a bobcat. Just as we ran into the store the owner banged the door so hard the cat was knocked senseless.

And my triumphant return home!! Well-fed, well-groomed, sitting on a chair in the huge green Studebaker wagon, holding my floral parasol aloft. I must have felt like a plump little princess returning to her home atop a canopied throne. Maybe it was the dosage of sassafras tea they first gave me that started me off so well, but the summer was a highlight in my store of memories.

One day my sister and I went on a children's picnic near a brook. Suddenly we came upon a large meadow emblazoned with wild flowers and there in the center stood a solitary tree completely enveloped by a wild rose vine. All the roses were in full bloom . . . such a beautiful memory. Pocahontas must have been in a lovely setting. In Dr. Pringle's yard stood a mimosa tree, the only one I've ever seen, a mass of tiny pinkish fluffy balls dipped in golden pollen. And the hickory nuts we used to crack on the sad iron clutched tightly between our knees. The nuts have a taste all their own and are worth the effort to dig them out of the hard shells. Beautiful fruitful Arkansas! Damp cold winters; hot, hot summers; spring rains; fall rains — but everything grew there and beauty abounded.

The reason I know it was cold in Pocahontas was the way we used to bundle up, long woolen underwear, flannel petticoat, black lisle stockings, black fleeced lined leggings that buttoned up — all tucked into buckled overshoes with spikes in the soles so we could get up and down the icy hills. We walked the mile or more to school and back. In warm weather we even came home for lunch. Four miles a day! A contrast to the car pools of today.

Maybe it was because I got frostbitten hands one winter or because the cotton crops of Forrest city seemed more lucrative than the apples and lumber of Pocahontas, but for some reason we moved again. Not until 1906 did we move.

I know we resided in Pocahontas when we all four attended the St. Louis World's Fair in 1904. My eyes must have bulged as I saw the "Shoot the Shoots" and the cascade where the finale of the ride was a boat shooting down a steep incline into a lagoon. How the women screamed as the boat hit the water! The lights and sound and music dazzled me. I'm still disappointed that I was left with my aunt while the older people really saw the shows and exhibitions. They dined at Faust's Restaurant. Thereafter Faust's coffee replaced the "Arbuckle's with chicory" we had used for years.

On one of Mama's reconnoitering trips for a better town, she returned home with a white dog. I guess Bully was a spitz, but we called him a Scotch-Irish poodle. How I loved that dog! I had to leave him behind while I went to St. Louis for some orthodontial work. In my absence the family moved to Forrest City, Arkansas, a town of about twenty-five hundred population. I only mention my dental work to record how advanced my mother was. Fifty years ago she knew about Dr. Lucas, a pioneer in this work. She cared enough to leave me with my aunt for eight months to improve my appearance.

Forrest City, spelled with two r's for [Confederate] General [Nathan Bedford] Forrest, was not a court square town. It had one long front street with business streets branching from it. Front Street ran parallel to the Rock Island Railway tracks which were bisected by the Iron Mountain Railway. The town was between Memphis and Little Rock. It was situated high upon Crowley's Ridge, but I don't recall it as a particularly hilly town.

We learned later how fortunate we were to be high. It was a cotton town and when the crops were good and the cotton all picked, business was most flourishing. Again, there were years of drought, years of boll weevil and horrible floods. All these catastrophes ruined the cotton and that fall would be bad. During the spring floods, when the melting snows of the north filled the St. Francis River to overflowing, I recall the refugees pouring in from the lowlands. It seemed more often than it probably was. Not only the farmers suffered, so did the merchants who had filled their shelves with merchandise and their hearts with high hopes. Some falls were bountiful, some tragically poor. It was a one season country — cotton picking time.

I do know my hardworking parents hadn't bettered themselves much by this move. I suddenly realized they may have done more, had they pooled their energies in one substantial store in St. Louis instead of going from one small Arkansas town to another. They may have attained more wealth. Mama's coercive salesmanship could have done much in more fertile fields. Yet on the third move it was better for them.

My parents may have struggled, but their children never knew it. Elocution lessons and piano lessons for me; piano and voice for my sister. We must have the education they couldn't get in Russia nor had time for in America, except for a brief period in night school. I think of them as newspaper educated, for both of them kept up zealously with current affairs; they knew a little about so many things. Mama could figure in her own way and come up with the answer before another could work it out with pencil and paper.

We certainly ate well in Forrest City. Those were the days when fryers were fifteen cents, two for twenty-five and a hen was thirty-five cents. Eggs, fifteen cents a dozen, and Elberta peaches (first grown and developed on Crowley's Ridge) were a dollar a bushel. Our number one salesman received $25.00 a week and we thought he was getting a fabulous salary — so did he.

Those were happy days for me, for all of us; we weren't rich but we lived comfortably, owned another white cottage on a plot of ground a quarter of a block square. It was in town but like a farm. Our yard had magnolia trees, sweet gum, black walnut, peach and pear, and a huge crab apple tree, plus a vegetable garden. Bessie the cow, Babe, my horse, Bully the dog, chickens and geese. One gander used to frighten me for he would hiss at me and chase me. Uncle Jim, an ex-slave, was our yard man. We had a cook and housemaid, all for less than what we now pay for two days work from a day worker. Maybe the help was exploited, but we fed them well and they seemed happy. Mother, even then, paid them more than the usual scale.

In Forrest City most homes had a separate servant's house. My mother nursed maids through small pox and pneumonia, attending to their needs as solicitously as she would to ours. Mama built no barriers! Her clerks called her Mother as time went by, even the customers called her Mother. One time a gray haired man called her that and she said. "There I draw the line." Mother had a terrific sense of humor and a hearty laugh. She was no longer petite — plump would be a generous word.

Darwin is right. I'm living proof of the theory. You couldn't keep this monkey out of trees, especially the magnolia trees. The magnolia wood is exceedingly brittle and is covered with a blackish powder, but very easy to climb. The first branches grow so high from the ground a ladder is required to get into a tree. Of course the most perfect blossoms and buds seemed to be at the very top of the tree. Always some neighbor or organization would want the beautiful blossoms for decorative purposes, and up I'd scramble to select the unblemished blossoms. I did it too often! When they phoned Mamma, I was on the ground and the doctor was on the way home. Mamma was at the dressmaker's, bless her heart, she ran out the front door and made the four blocks before they had me off the ground — only she forgot to put on her dress. There she was in an allover embroidered corset cover and a voluminous starched petticoat, more effective covering than today's underwear.

My sister was always occupied with a novel, school books or work in the store, but once in Pocahontas she outclimbed me. She was fascinated by the metal steps on a telephone pole. Papa came along just as she had reached the top rung. She looked down and became frozen to the pole — she couldn't climb down. Quietly Papa guided her and coaxed her down. Once she was safely on the ground she got her spanking. It must have been a good one for her climbing days ended before they were well begun.

The summers were beastly hot in St. Francis County. With chagrin I now recall how we were allowed to spend our days; breakfast in bed lying around in the hammock that hung between the magnolia trees until it got cool enough to dress and meander into town for our daily ice cream soda. When it was cool enough, we'd ride our horses or play with our friends. Oh, we were not entirely useless. When the busy fall came, we'd help in the store, and do it willingly. It's just that the summers were hot and business was dull. Forrest City was a Saturday town. But our parents were in the store, hot or not. Maybe they were even cooler than we under the large ceiling electric fans of the times.

Somehow, no matter how small the community, we always found many educated and interesting people. One such find in Forrest City was Dr. Mabley and his wife and four children. He was an Episcopal minister, direct from Oxford University. He was American, but his wife and children were British. Mother always recognized quality when she saw it and was delighted when Sarah and I became friendly with these children. The real closeness was between Annie Mabley and my sister.

Each Passover season the Mabley family en masse and any single man or woman of our faith would share the seder meal with us. Usually the father tells the story of Moses and the Exodus from Egypt, but Dr. Mabley did it so brilliantly each year he was the narrator. First the story and the wine and symbolic food: the matzos, the hard boiled egg, the bitter herb, the *horasious* (that delicious apple and wine and cinnamon combination that represents the bricks the Jews made in Egypt) and then the late dinner. First Gefilte fish, then matzo balls in chicken soup, then the meat and *tzimmas,* a festive concoction of prunes, carrots and potatoes, and the pudding and cakes made of matzo meal. At the end of that dinner we'd all be stuffed and lethargic. But it is the one religious festival I relish best because it was Mama's supreme effort of the year.

Mama was too busy to cook much, except on Sundays. And how I hated those cooking Sundays. No one could dirty as many pots and pans as she could. It was the help's day off and all I did was wash dishes all day long. Mama would make blintzes, thin pancakes filled with cheese and fried in butter or knishes, raised dough filled with ground meat and fried onions and baked, or *veronikas,* noodle dough filled with buckwheat and onions and ground meat. These were steamed and served dripping with gravy or chicken fat. Delicious, you can be sure, but no wonder Mama was fat. She'd prepare these European dishes and serve them to whoever dropped in.

And drop in they did. I learned to call our home the Wayside Inn. Forrest City was a railway junction and all the co-religionists from nearby towns going to Memphis or Little Rock or St. Louis had to come through our town and always called on us. In later years when the auto came, they'd assemble in Forrest City for inter-community picnics. Don't think people in small towns don't enjoy themselves. Picnics with scads of fried chicken, ice cold watermelons, etc. were very frequent in those days.

The main hotel, operated by the Rock Island Railway was old, so it seemed we frequently had travelers sleeping with us. Maybe because very early in the picture we had one of the few bathtubs in town. The privy (as it was called) was still a little wooden house away at the far end of the garden. Somewhere along here the closed sewage came to us and with it the flush toilet. I can't recall exactly when. And now we burned soft coal in our fancy stoves trimmed with a lot of nickle plate. The parlor and one bedroom were heated by fireplaces and never really got hot in the winter.

I lost a year of school in St. Louis and was entered in the third grade in Forrest City where I continued with my schooling through high school. When my sister reached high school age Dr. Mabley realized the standard of high school teaching was not too good, so he undertook to tutor his daughter and Sarah. Fortunate girls! After they completed their training they both tested themselves by attending Teacher's Institute and passing at the very top of the class. Annie completed her higher education in St. Louis and Sarah went to New

York for a year, then to Boston to the New England Conservatory of Music. There Sarah became Selma.

How many of us nostalgically recall the gathering of our particular gang in one yard or another. We played London Bridge or tag. Hide and Seek and even Drop the Hankerchief. Then we grew a little older and paired off. Post Office became popular and Spin the Plate, even Crack-the-Whip, and picnics where our special boy would carve two pairs of initials in a heart on some blackwood tree. Who thought of juvenile delinquents then or restless teenagers? We were too occupied. Some few even played tennis, the new game, but best of all was horseback riding — my best pet and friend was Babe, my gray mare, whom I used to curry and brush and saddle myself. She was my charge. I guess Uncle Jim was always standing by because she stayed well groomed.

In Forrest City in 1910 to 1914 my friends and I never knew of being restless and maladjusted. If we weren't picnicking or playing games, we'd go to the various lumber mills and learn by asking a lot of questions. Another trip was to the spoke mill where wagon wheel spokes were cut, also bannister spokes for fancy stairways. On one such excursion we watched them process a rough log into planks. There always seemed to be adequate diversion for our absorbent minds. And the lumber supply of the delta country produced many things. There was also a barrel mill we liked to visit. I remember St. Francis County best as farming country, but lumber must have also played its part.

The County Agent was no doubt a new thing then. I recall hearing much talk of diversification. "Plant sweet potatoes and peanuts, not only cotton" was the most often heard phrase. Well may they have planted more lucious yellow yams and mushy Nancy Hall sweet potatoes, for I can't think of anything more appealing than the soft sweet potatoes of Arkansas.

The Jewish population of Forrest City was too small for a congregation, so we visited other churches. A fine Methodist minister used to notify my parents that he would preach an Old Testament sermon about Abraham or Moses or the prophets and we'd show up that Sunday to get some Bible education. I'd often go to prayer meeting with Willie Mae Sanders to the Baptist Church. One year when I was fourteen I got rebellious. I wanted a service of our own. I wrote Rabbi

Samuels [Rabbi Max Samfield] in Memphis about my desire to have the ten or twelve children of our faith attend their own Sabbath School. He sent me material and from then on the lessons were held each Sunday morning in our home. My father gave me the fill-in instruction I needed. Dr. Samuels organized the men also. From then on a cantor was hired for the high holidays, Rosh Hashonah to Yom Kippur, and we proudly attended our own services.

Not even the rural South lacked its share
of Jewish immigrants, though they were never numerous in that region.
Jeannette Warshavsky Bernstein recalls the experience
of her family in northeastern Arkansas around the turn of the century.

My Own Story

Bessie Schwartz

In 1886, I was born in the little town of Podu Turculu, Rumania. It was a picturesque town — lots of trees, bushes and the river. Some of the village people did their washing at the river bank; no wash board; just washing the garment from one hand to the other. The clothes came out surprisingly clean. As a young child, I enjoyed watching them do it until the washing was done. After the water settled in the river, the cows and sheep were brought for a drink.

The town of Podu Turculu was small; it had two streets. One lane was called the Crooked Street. We had a nice river, also the central market place for buying and selling. Once — my sister Anna was then only ten days old — the whole town burned down, and all the people went down to the river with their scant belongings. We were very fortunate that the wheat elevator, which my father owned, was undamaged, but our home was gone. Luckily, no lives were lost. But in the terrible excitement during the fire, Anna, the baby, was dragged with her head down, feet up, until our place was found. Looking back, it seems a touch of comedy.

The country there was very interesting, as it raised much fruit, especially grapes. Then again in European countries, where various nationalities live so close to one another, we used to have people from all the other countries visit us. The Bulgarians especially are wonderful gardeners; the Turks with their good coffee, made in coppermills, wore red fezzes and white belts at the waistlines.

There were lots of gypsies from throughout the Balkan countries; the superstitiousness of our people has always been evident in their turning to the gypsies for guidance. The climate in Rumania is quite mild, lots of heavy snow, but less frost. On some holiday celebrations, we used to go into the woods and there we would roast a young lamb over a charcoal flame. As children we loved it. The scent and the taste of that time still seem to be with me. Of course, we were given all the wine we wished — even the children drank wine as we drink water. It was an area for wineries. Wine was used as a medicinal protector, since our water was polluted, unclean.

I went to school four grades there — about the same in standard as the eight grades here. For extra languages, tutors were necessary to learn German, French, and English. I had a few German lessons and learned some nursery songs and poems.

By the time I was twelve, the family had grown bigger in size and poorer in money; I was the eldest of seven children. Now came the time to think of moving to America. My father did not want his sons to do military training — compulsory in Rumania — so his only longing and wishing was to go to America, a free land for everyone. The relatives who had preceded us had encouraging tales of opportunities here — plus all the hardships the newcomer must face. By that time, however, we were so many. One of my mother's brothers lent the money needed for tickets — for steerage class — for all of us. This uncle lent the money without his wife's knowledge, but he was repaid later with good interest.

All we took along was the bedding, the silver, and our few clothes. Some of my mother's earliest housekeeping tools, such as old brass and copper pieces, candelabra, and coffee mills are our prizes today.

From our village, we had to go to Berlad, where we boarded the third class section of the Orient Express (wooden seats; and we carried our own sacks of food) via Vienna and Germany to Rotterdam, Holland — all this in October, 1901. In Holland, the wooden shoes were of interest, also the different food delicacies. Aboard the ship, we had our first taste of doing something for ourselves — we had to prepare and take care of our toilet habits aboard ship (clean clothes, shampoo hair, polish shoes). As small children in Rumania, we always had help available for every little job. The English people on the ship were fine military men; for amusement, they threw us children coins down to the steerage class. We thought money in America must be easy to get if that was the way it was used. But the trip across was not easy; we were seven children and two parents, with a dozen or more bundles tied about us. In boarding the ship, during the counting of the members of the family, plus the bundles, a strange lucky kid came along with us. My father gave this lonely fourteen year old boy a big push and he was in with us. The ship's steward and my father each counted in his own way—but stay with us he did, until we reached Toronto.

We entered North America via Montreal and Quebec, stopping in Toronto, and reached Minneapolis—the Milwaukee Station—with masses of smiling relatives awaiting us. The station was beautiful and brand new.

One cousin, Ben Rigler, said to my father, "What are you to me?" in poor Yiddish. My father was surprised that the young men and women here knew so little Yiddish.

This was a beautiful America, but life was more difficult and so much different for us than in Rumania. Here we had to work; we knew no English; we had to move faster, quicker, go longer distances, and do jobs for which we had had no training and had never thought of doing. My mother had to learn to do her own washing (we had always had help in Europe); and my father had to get used to a horse and wagon and become a merchant on the street. They were called fruit peddlers. The horse used to run away. At home, Father never had known how to use or care for a horse; he had a couple of bad accidents too. It became unbearable for him. On the other hand, most of the children started school and worked before and after school selling newspapers—walking miles to receive their bundles. All the earnings went into the family fund. But—the American pies—what a wonderful new thing for us.

I unfortunately went to school just to the fourth grade here in the United States. There were too many difficulties and unhappy times and also unresourceful parents, who didn't care too much whether I attended or not. My father was restless with his life as a peddler here in this city, but for a while that situation continued. In Europe he had been a grain merchant and had prospered in a small way. But now, by this time, the seven children had grown into ten children. He always used to say "My load of family is very heavy," and yet he dreamed of educating his family, because his own childhood education (he had been left an orphan) had been meager and poor. This was not for me, nor for the two brothers, Charles and Ben—the rest were helped and continued in their schooling—I dropped out. It was not easy for me, not knowing the language. My parents, especially my mother, refused to learn English. She continued her speech and her customs and manners in Yiddish only. On that account we lost out some; she the most. This stubborn habit made life more difficult for us — we could not go forward too much. Amazingly, we had lots of will power, necessity forcing us to use other methods and means to learn. So I ventured out and became a cash girl.

In those days, for a foreign girl unlearned in American ways, this achievement was a big feather in my cap. Time went on — we were a happy lot. Only the most in planning and fixing came to me first; being the eldest may bring some glories, but most of all the worries. I could not change that situation. I never knew a vacation, just talked of a future one.

We lived on 5th Street and 12th Avenue South. When I was about sixteen years old — tall, fair, slender, not bad in looks — one Sunday afternoon Max (my future husband), also not bad looking, stylishly dressed with a bow tie and brown plaid suit, came to us to exchange greetings from his parents with my grandmother, who had come with them from Europe. The first thing my mother said to me, "Go and get a dish with fruit, especially the good-looking bananas, that Grandpa brought home." I served the young man, and the food brought the words right out of his mouth. We became acquainted.

I became a clerk in ready-to-wear apparel at the Leader Department Store. I must say I was a number one sales clerk. I felt very big to be one, and with everything so difficult in those days, we all did a good job. We did have a fighting spirit in us. The days of yesterday with a dry lunch under the arm, the dessert — a five cent cup of hot chocolate, were great and happy days. All walked to work, by the train tracks to have a shorter route to and from home. Our longest work day was Saturday, from early morning until ten o'clock each night. By that time, Max, my boy friend, came to get me — we walked home with a ten cent bag of candy. When we reached home, Mother was ready with some prepared food to serve us. We didn't go to night clubs, nor cafes for refreshment. We really had a feeling of hope. We started to think about our future; plans couldn't be made because we had no money.

———————

I was still vacation conscious, so in order to get one, we discussed the job of taking homesteads (then being offered by Uncle Sam) for our start in life. So a half dozen of our two families ventured out to southwestern North Dakota, to a miserable area — six pieces of land, one hundred and sixty acres for each one. We filed our claim for this land, which had no water and was covered with stones, debris from the strong winds and storms. No towns were nearby. We had to remain on the land at least nine months before we would be entitled to the deed.

A new hardship: I had never been away from home and also had very little money to make this miserable land more attractive. It was very hard for me to venture out, but still I wished to do it. The country was wild, bare, coyotes all over like little wolves. The coyotes live in the ground. We crossed the country with horses and a wagon, full of movable articles and lumber. The womenfolk crossed the river on bare feet; the memory is still with me, just like the gypsy of yesterday. We finally got there. Each person had to have so much in improvements on his land; each one had a one room house built on his claim. The interior was of lumber; the exterior, for warmth, was of sod. It was nice and warm. The furniture consisted of a bed, stove, trunk, shelves on the walls. I myself dug out a two foot cellar, to keep milk cold and butter, too, in a pail of water.

Our facilities: we didn't have any ice or hygienic systems or plumbing. We had a water pool, where the cattle gathered to drink; after that water settled, we took it and sterilized it for our own drinking water. I made a beautiful garden—and I had never known how to grow a radish; the garden was beautiful, until we had a thunderstorm, and everything was completely cut off. Our small hut houses were all turned upside down. Imagine how we all looked and felt. And I was so terribly homesick besides—the first vacation and the first removal from family ties.

Max used to help the neighbors with the haying, and we girls used to embroider small articles and attempt some cooking. We filled up the hope chests with embroidered articles. Oh yes, when I went out to North Dakota, my father gave me a horse. I thought a horse would help my vacation. The horse wasn't worth much of anything, but I got the satisfaction of learning how to ride a little—without a saddle, with but a rug underneath me. All the horse did was to take me three quarters of a mile to get the mail; we sold it for five dollars.

Before the womenfolk went out to the homesteads, the men usually went ahead to build the houses (called shacks). In the beginning, Dad (my husband) and Uncle Hash Rigler (Leo's father) landed there. Tired—no water was in sight on that plain wild prairie—they took two pails and went hunting for a place with water, walking all these miles on the stony, lonely prairie. At last they found a slough with some left over rain water, gathered this water, after chasing the animals out, and got the two pails of water. Little was left after the long return walk. They got lost and walked and walked — they finally made it by dusk. They barely recognized their place; in exhaustion they went to sleep in their tent and by morning they found the whole tent covered with snow. Those were the early days. I even watched cowboys breaking in the wild horses and branding horses and cattle too. It was quite an experience for me.

On a homestead one has many experiences; I tried my cooking and baking for my future life as a wife. My uncle, Hash Rigler, taught me how to bake bread, but without measurements. I made enough bread to last for many days, as he kept on saying "Add more water. Add more flour." The worst part of it, was to bake it in an oven attached to the smoking stove pipe. One should have received the first prize in baking bread there. And it was good too, in spite of everything.

My Aunt Rose and Uncle Osias had their homestead within half a mile from mine; so they had a grocery store just for neighbors around there. They had a horse and buggy. One day I decided to borrow that horse and buggy for an errand, but did not know that the horse had to have a bridle in his mouth. The moment I took the reins, the horse with no bridle in the mouth, began to run; I in the buggy yelled and yelled for help. Fortunately, several customers were going toward the store at that time, but the horse made up his mind to get rid of me and run back to the barn. So he did that: threw me out, one foot away from a forty-foot open well. Lucky me, I came out all right. Just before I fell, my aunt ran out to soothe the horse with some soft talk, "Johnny Dear, Johnny Stop" — but this Johnny Dear threw me off instead and went into the barn.

Yes, our pioneering days left us with great memories. I really can't see how we did it, but we did live through it. One night looking for Max (out haying, he wasn't back before dark) my future sister-in-law, Rose, and I were very worried, so we decided we would walk in the direction of the store, even though it was already dark out.

The only protection we had was a revolver. Rose was against taking it, because I might kill Max by mistake. So I took a long pole, and Rose took a candle. I took the forward steps and when we got up on the hill, we both saw a spot on the road. She was older but she said, "Bessie, do you see something?" To keep a brave front, I said, "Oh, I saw it long ago—watch me hit it." When I hit the spot hard, it was nothing but a bundle of hay, and all I said was, "Didn't I tell you so." Meanwhile the little coyotes were yelling and we arrived at the store where we found Max and the rest all well. Yes, the western world had lots of experiences for man's pioneering days. That's what made the men of today.

Time went on—soon it would be time to prove up the land and return to Minnesota. I was sick and homesick. We had put in all the improvements; the well, house, hut, and fence wiring and paid Uncle Sam $1.25 per acre, and we had such poor land. From within our closely knit community in Minneapolis, I was the first Jewish girl to try something like this. Actually, the homesteads proved to be something of a family village, with so many members settling each group. The houses were built with little outside help; the interiors were all about the same.

Among the homesteaders were three future sisters-in-law (two married and one single). One sister-in-law, Hinda, was a widow with three children. She was very pious and religious in household customs; since she would eat only kosher food, she lived as a vegetarian for eleven months. Her children were young; a boy in his teens working with relatives, a small nine year old boy named Martin, and a little girl of six named Rebecca. Martin had a dog. One day both Martin and the dog disappeared. We looked all over the countryside, until darkness came. By midnight the exhausted Martin was dragged home by his dog—to the joy of all. There had been fear of prairie coyotes.

One day Hinda became very sick and to get the doctor there just was not possible. One had to take the patient by horse and wagon to the doctor over many rough miles. We barely made it. She refused to go at first, with "I was never sick in my life—why did it have to happen to me now?" She recovered, but the rest of her life was hard, with no pleasures of any kind, she died in Minneapolis when only sixty-two years old.

I had more energy than the rest of the women. Time didn't mean anything. My Uncle Hash and I were neighbors. His claim was a quarter of a mile up the hill, and mine was in the valley below. His son, nine year old Leo, came to my rescue the nights I was most disturbed by field mice. He would spend the nights with me—I would frighten him during the night over the noise of the mice. Half asleep, he would say. "Where is he? I shall get him." Who would have thought that this little fellow would become a nationally famous doctor, a professor of radiology at the University Hospital.

On the homestead, for recreation, were the country dances; we went and returned on the hay racks early in the morning. Before returning home, we had breakfast with the cowboys—they were the cooks, making pancakes with unwashed hands. I was even frightened of the cowboys with their pistols. They talked and spit as fast as they used the guns: and me from a city, how upset I was. How different we have it today.

We saw the land wasn't much good, but we had to make the best of it. We had great hopes that this adventure would help us for the future. We proved up in Bowman, North Dakota, and a railroad was built during our stay, six miles from our land. I was the first one to go home. Not only was I glad to go, all were glad to see me go—sick and homesick. By the way, Max had a few hundred dollars when he went out to North Dakota, but he had to borrow some more by the time we proved up the land.

The place where I had to take the train—a plain prairie—the train had to be flagged down. The building, once meant to become a hotel, had only a roof and a floor with a few cots, with tired men resting. The two sisters and brother that supervised this building never returned from their dance until 4:30 a.m. and I had a book in my hands, but who read it? My thoughts were frightening, watching the men sleep. I was teased too. They asked me to rest, but I told them I just was interested in my book. The owners returned just when the train arrived, practically at the same time. My face was not pale; it was white with fright—and yet this all was a great experience. Maybe, years later, that's why my own family got the urge to travel young.

After a few months at home, I went to work as a saleslady. Six months later, Max and I decided to get married. I didn't get any raise in my weekly pay of hard work, and I became tired of constant promises. At that point, I took courage and went out to one of the finest stores on Nicollet Avenue—The Young-Quinlan Company. I felt I could always put over a good sale on clothes, and why not work in a fancy store with more pay? Besides I needed the money for the wedding. I always said to myself, "All they could do, is say No."

Other girls could speak English better, but I had the courage. It took nerve to ask, and to my surprise, I was told they would let me know soon. A few days later, back at my usual job at The Leader, a special delivery messenger came up looking for Miss Halpern. To my surprise, the floorwalker took the note and handed it to me. And before I even opened the envelope, he said, "If Young's are after you, we won't let you go." So I said, "I will go regardless, because I need money, and I plan to get married." He said that in the next pay check a raise would show up — so I stayed and got $10 a week instead of $6 and made a little extra (25 cents per garment) on old stock. But I was happy because it was my own doing and I was not afraid.

The wedding was to take place the 12th of July, 1908. It was quite something. I was not in favor of a large wedding; my parents felt otherwise, and their excuse was that I was the eldest, and they wanted everybody — the butcher, the baker, the candlestick maker; all their European friends and relatives, then my friends; we had over 200 people against my wishes. The best part of it, my father took a loan to pay for this big unnecessary wedding and included wine, dinner, and dancing. We had two rabbis to perform the service to please both families; to make a better, stronger wedding. One thing I was satisfied about — I made a good looking bride and left the worries to the planners. My wedding gown was from New York, all white lace and a beautiful bouquet of flowers; all the fancy dresses for the girls (sisters-bridesmaids) were made by a dressmaker. The wedding was a gay occasion, with the police as our guests after returning from the dance hall. The next step was our future move to Dickinson, North Dakota, where Max was going into the cigar business with a Mr. Tobias.

The honeymoon was on the coach train (I think green plush) enroute to Dickinson. We had no berth for two reasons; one — no money, and two, we had a big statue with two big wings, a gift from the employees of The Leader store. So Max and I took turns holding the statue for some 600 miles on our laps. That's how I remember the honeymoon. At that time I weighed 119 pounds and today at 68 years, I am 162. We went to Dickinson to start in the cigar business; it wasn't much, but we tried it for a couple years. A year later, Charlotte, the eldest daughter was born, but I went to Minneapolis for that event. My parents were still living in this city, but a year or two later, they too moved out to a small Dakota town — Hebron.

It was time to do something for ourselves. With my father's encouragement and help, and some interest in the project by other Dickinson relatives, we decided to become merchants. Max picked out a small place 20 miles west of Dickinson, called Belfield, with 500 people living there. This was it — mud up to the knees, not a light on the street. So we, the Schwartzes, put up the first tall kerosene lamp post. The weekly newspaper covered two thirds of the news with that topic — everyone was so delighted. Right in front of this western store, we had horse posts to accommodate the customers, and the western ranch boys made good use of them too. They drove up in front; horses stood still awaiting their masters. That was something new for me. At that time the horses were smarter than the people. During those days, many foreign people traded with us; Ukrainians, Bohemians, Russians, Germans, and Scandinavians. As I was a young bride and shy when I entered the store, I never had a feeling that I should speak to people without an introduction. One time my husband spoke up and told me I didn't need an introduction if I wanted a customer in the store. The saying was, "Keep what you have, until you get what you want." The art of living is the art of using your own experience and knowledge gained from other people. The whole town admired us, especially our store, with its city touch of helping out the customers, even in choosing the patterns and styles for sewing.

We listened to all the folks' tales of their family problems, sickness, troubles. We became old-fashioned listeners. We were good for that and became friends with our customers. In the back of the store, we allotted a space for the farm trade to make and serve themselves with their own lunches; it was a help for them with all their babies. We were thought quite remarkable; they were devoted to us, and we were glad.

Our store was located on the south side, separated by the railroad tracks from the rest of the town. We had an old time heavy wooden sidewalk, from the tracks to the store. We lived in six rooms and a small porch attached to the store. We had a sink in the kitchen with a pump. Water for washing came from the cistern, and we always had soft water. The drinking water was either carried in pails from a well across the tracks, or put into milk cans. How we survived I do not know. We took baths in the wash tub; in the summer, the water was warmed outdoors, in the winter on the old black stove (we had a beautiful self-heater in the living room; lots of work to that beauty with all its nickel plating). We pulled the tub in the house for the Saturday night baths. This was the usual picture in the early mornings: My husband built the fire in the kitchen with wood and soft coal and opened the oven to heat the room; we had two high-chairs for the babies, and they would sit and watch the flames. Max would have made the coffee by that time; the children then dressed. Not until many years later did we have a telephone; before that I knocked on the wall and could notify my husband that way when the meals were ready. The store hours were from 7:30 A.M. to 9 P.M. each day: on Saturday until after 10 P.M.

Our help was sent for from Minneapolis or thereabouts; we had hoped to get some men with experience. When they did come out, these men refused to eat in the restaurants and insisted on living and eating with us — quite a job with a growing family and no easy plumbing or running water or heat. I was young in thought and experience. I used to say to the boys that stayed with us, "What shall I cook for tomorrow?" The answer was, "Anything is better than we would get downtown."

One young man, Ben Neff, came to us when the children were very young; a splendid looking fellow, full of life but all alone in the United States; a few members of his family were in Russia. Ben really lived all the years around us. He is still one of our oldest friends and spends many a holiday with either my daughter Alice or here with us. He enjoyed the small town work, some of the gay dances, and the people liked him. He was a fine salesman, humored the customers, was friendly with everyone. These years he gives much of his time to the various veterans' organizations — servicing them in the same way he once was helped. Another young man, much remembered, was Ignace Kushner, who unhappily lost his life in World War I in France. Then there was our nephew — Hinda's elder son, Louis Abern. He too was liked by everyone and seemed happy there; he played on the baseball team and remained with us until a better opportunity came his way. The help had to learn to understand and speak a little of the Russian language — most of the farmers at that time in that area were of the first generation and knew no English.

As a rule the small town had Saturday night dances. When I dressed

— always in a rush — I had to run back into the store for some bit of finery for myself; a flower, or a ribbon maybe. We were young, but sometimes we had to miss some of the dances. People plagued us about that. And when we did go, we once tried it out with the eldest child, taking her along. We placed her in the hall on two chairs, and she slept all through it. We loved to square dance wearing the bright Ukrainian shawls.

Can you visualize an old time country store? A stove in the center of the store, a couple of large spittoons around it, men chewing their tobacco and spitting into the spittoons, eating peanuts and throwing them into the stove. The best gathering place was around the stove. Old time stories were told by the customers to each other and to us, and we never stayed idle. We strung stockings and handkerchiefs into bundles and put them on a line on the ceiling. This seemed the easiest way for the customers, but not for us. Being in the store, I remember a lot of things. Most of the customers talked a lot, but to be tactful and better for business, silence on our part was best. We just took the thought home and slept on it. By that time, a good friendship was started.

After lunch time, with the children off to school, I used to have an old German woman, Mrs. Pauline Kruser, who would take over my duties in watching the two babies and help clean up. She often took the small boys home with her, while I played sales lady in the store. To me this was a great "outlet," a different picture of life. I was dressed up. I was busy, but it was a sort of recreation too, until it was time to make the supper. This was a daily job. There were times when we had different help too, but no one was as dependable with the children as Mrs. Kruser.

We had one particularly close family relationship with the Mike Donoghue Family. It seems that the Catholic Irish and the Jewish families get along very well. They were very witty, and told many a story of the Irish famine and their own railroad problems. Mr. Donoghue and the sons all worked for the Northern Pacific Railroad, from the early days since James J. Hill started the Northern Pacific Railway. The reason Mr. Donoghue had so much time — he was paralyzed from a bad accident in the boiler house. For eight years he lived in bed, cared for by his wife and daughter Annie. He still had his lively old time gags for us all. Each evening I would visit them for a little while. Annie was my best friend all the years we were there — until her death in 1927.

Talking of honesty — we had a steady clerk by the name of Ase Thomas. He worked for us a number of years. To my husband's surprise — Ase made change at the register — he noticed that Ase continually made a motion toward his left side pocket. Some change went into that pocket. Max was very shocked. He stopped him right there, and only asked him how long he had been doing that. At that particular time, he had taken $20. Ase thought he was fired from the job. He said he did this daily for small change. Max told him to stop this dishonesty and he could still keep his job.

I wish I could make you see the sort of pastimes that made for happiness. Sometimes I would make up a batch of doughnuts and go sixty miles to visit my parents in Hebron, and we would eat by the creek. The flies and their poisons: no flies were like those found in Hebron. I still marvel that the children never got an infection from them.

The little things counted most for us. We never failed in business, no matter how hard the going. We always came through. Credit doesn't just pay up bills; it's the honesty of it. One day a middle aged couple came in to purchase their groceries and, in the midst of the busy hours, paid their bill and went across to the Northside Post Office and Bank. We discovered a pouch with $200 in it; our honesty followed the couple and gave them back their money. With the greatest joy they thanked us and never forgot us. On the other hand, we gave out a lot of charge credit; quite a percentage never did pay up.

For example: once a Mr. Chesky came to see my husband; he used to take the annual inventory in Belfield. He cornered my husband and told him something was bothering him very much, that he had a confession to make — and wished to pay in full. He told him that years before whenever he had purchased a box of groceries from us he took them home through the back door, and on the way out, would help himself to one or two hams hanging from the ceiling. My husband refused to take the money and told him to forget it, it had happened so long ago.

All Max talked about in the early days was having good credit. He seemed to hold that above all else. It isn't always easy to answer a customer when he asks if the merchandise can be charged. This meant us and in turn our customers too. Our great thrill was being given merchandise easily. One must work and earn this credit; we had had nothing to start with, and we were young. The credit bureau is your boss. We had to depend on our knowledge of arithmetic. The returns gave us the most satisfaction.

We had a big straw rocking chair, and I rocked two babies at the same time and kept watching the few trains a day through the window. The best thing for my mind was to count the freight trains, while putting the children to sleep. My life was not a quiet life; the older girls were busy with piano lessons and school doings. Then later we had to send them to Dickinson by train for lessons. Small places did not have much to offer—not even a library. There were no movies in the early years. The boys were more mischievous. Frank was once lost at an early age after the store was closed. It was almost night. We looked all over town, even in the reservoir, and found no trace of him. Finally, I thought we might have locked him up in the store, and we tried that. We found him sitting inside of a bin, full of raisins, not a bit unhappy. What a sweet scare. Then, when Gerald was two years old, we lost him. He used to go to the cistern and throw in his shoes—20 feet deep. We surely thought he was there—but instead he was found asleep in an unpacked merchandise box outdoors. The sport for the winter season was to take the children sliding up and down the hills. We also had a beautiful creek with seven little bridges just like European villages. Our town consisted of many different churches and we had good ball games. Most of the people were dressed in western clothes, especially the men. We used to sell fine quality hats, jackets, and boots. The western handkerchiefs, the gay Russian scarfs—I never will forget them.

We kept up the stock of the store in fine shape. The butter used to be bought in chunks and put into barrels. We didn't have creamery butter then. The winters are to be remembered. It may not sound right, but one bad winter we had 40 degrees below. Everything was calm and quiet, but within twenty-four hours we had a heavy rain.

Life was pleasant in the warm months; we had visitors from out of town; we were always complimented on the good care given to our little house. After supper, with the children asleep, the men sat around the table with the newspaper, while I was always fixing and mending garments, and many garments for my mother too. Some of my brothers and sisters wore the same type and size clothing as my children. Sometimes a young brother or sister spent months with us. I used to walk a lot, watching our neighbors trying to get water out of the dry wells. There were the heavy clouds; sagebrush; the land was very flat, and yet the Western character always had the feeling that tomorrow would be a better day. The last few seasons — no crops; locusts or dust took over. I lived there many a dry year. Later, the dams were built, and the water was distributed — all this helped this area so much.

The change of transportation has brought many changes in this forgotten dry land. Now with good cars and highway concerts are brought to the larger cities; lectures arranged and willingly paid for; some theatre groups invited out; and more interest in native culture and crafts has brought attention local and national. The people there are skeptical of their good fortune, however, and keep wondering how long this will last. It is an old saying that Americans love a hard country, but the West must be loved as you love your family.

There were twelve brothers and sisters in my family — in order of age: Bessie, Charles, Ben, Samuel, Anna, Esther, Ruth, Saul, Frances, Blanche, Maurice, and Tobette. Tobette and my second daughter, Alice, are the same age; in fact, Toby is three months younger. Saul — one of the younger brothers — in his early teens spent some time with me, when I was a bride in Dickinson. Mother just turned his rheumatic sickness over to me, whether I knew anything about it or not. Instead of being in bed, the lively little Saul jumped from one chair to another. I had to put up with him; we took over the parents' duties. My brothers were all spoiled; the parents were much more partial to them. They never picked up their own clothes, or helped in home duties — left to the girls, especially me, the oldest. My grandmother was blind for twenty-five years; she got along fine, because Grandpa did not work outside the home, but helped her a bit. We, the grandchildren, were at her side very much; we liked her for her smartness and shrewdness. She was the one who felt bad when I quit school so young and could not go further. If Mother would have been a better manager, I could have finished the public school at least. My father provided sufficiently in a very modest way. Mother missed the constant European help around her — I was quick, so why not?

During my parents' years in Hebron, I was often called home to come with the next train. Once my father had swallowed a piece of glass, found in a baker's loaf of bread. I went down with two tiny babies. I had the responsibility of the store and the household; my parents had gone to the city for medical help. One night I decided to make small brown beans. All liked them, except Saul. He kicked it all around; I said, "By the time I say 1-2-3, eat this." Instead, he made a face, and I fired it all out with the plate and all. Then he was sore, and picked up a large dish-pan with all the dirty dishes, and threw the whole pan down, breaking everything. In turn I spanked him with a coat hanger. All he said was that he would remember this tale when I too had children and this had all been paid off.

For dental services, we went to Dickinson, and occasionally to Bismarck (130 miles) by train. Many a holiday like Easter, Thanksgiving, and Christmas meant going to Hebron to join my folks. I went a few days earlier to help prepare the festivities for the rest of the family. All the children and grandchildren came — sleeping room was tight; children were placed in the width — three or four to a bed. Each bedroom had two large beds; there were four bedrooms and a very large sleeping porch. This home was built by my parents, and it had all the modern conveniences. They were very proud of it. In those days, this was quite an accomplishment. When we ran out of chairs around the table, we used long boards for seats. During those days, one of my brothers, Samuel, was taking law at the University of North Dakota, and he would come home for the holidays; and all that his work consisted of was checking the amount of sales and money in the cash register.

I had another brother, Charles, who lived in New England. Charles is the brother next to me, and he and a cousin, Betty Rigler, were married a year and a half after our marriage. We went down to attend their wedding with the baby Charlotte to Minneapolis. After many years in New England, Charlie and Betty moved to Los Angeles, where they are enjoying three sons, eight grandchildren, and sunny days.

Anna (my sister) and her husband Charles Rosen lived in Bismarck; my brother, Ben, in Golden Valley; we in Belfield; two half-uncles were in Glen Ullin, two aunts in Dickinson. Those in Glen Ullin were half-brothers to my father. They were rather different than us in that they wished money more than anything else. One year, when another young brother-in-law (my husband's brother Dave) was to be married in Bismarck, nearly everyone was invited to this large hotel wedding. We drove there, stopping in Glen Ullin on the way; we asked the families there if they weren't coming too. Molly said, "Maybe yes, maybe no; we have coats, new dresses, and also our diamond rings (newly purchased). But on second thought, why should we go? We think Dave Schwartz can get married without us, so goodbye, goodbye." How funny.

We had so little social life that each occasion was made into an event. We had several lodges; the Odd Fellows, Rebeccas, and Royal Neighbors, and the Eastern Star in Dickinson. We had dances, meetings, and of course the evening refreshments. The annual banquet used to be the outstanding event, especially the hunting season. The wild birds made a wonderful dinner — a couple of breasts for each person. During the years from 1910 to 1915, we happened to get quite a few young newlywed couples in Belfield. They always used to parade on the old wooden sidewalk from the northside of town to the South Side Cash Store. They always used to say, "If we can't find the article at the South Side, then we must go to Dickinson." I used to make and trim our display windows, and do other jobs to make the place more attractive. I also had to please my husband, with my appearance, home duties or not. He always has been too particular, especially about my hair and I had to have my pompadour done up just so. When he introduced me to the salesmen, he was glad of a good appearance.

My own brothers and sisters all remember these days very well. When our New Year High Holidays came along, all the Jewish communities from the surrounding towns near Dickinson went there for the few days. Each family donated financial help each year until a small synagogue was built and paid for, including all the sacred articles. The holiday gathering was more than a religious soul-searching; it was the time for exchange of sociabilities, fellowship and good feeling; all stayed at the St. Charles or Villard Hotels. The managers of both hotels had hearty souls and kind hearts.

The best clothes and best foods were brought along either by car or train. Meals were eaten together. After the Yom Kippur Holy Day, and the breaking of the fast, came the Annual Ball at the country club, where everyone, adult, child, and baby, had a happy time before departing for the various homes in the early morning hours. Since those years, most of the Jewish people who had originally built this synagogue have moved elsewhere. The synagogue building was sold, and the sacred articles were given to the Bismarck Temple.

I think North Dakota was nice to all of us, but we used to envy the Minnesota greenery and trees — we were without knowledge or desire to develop any ourselves. Of course, we were short of water and much of our soil was of alkali content, but perhaps we could have tried to make more beauty. We didn't have much gardening endurance or patience either.

We felt close to the people we met and got to know out there. We had to make something out of nothing; picnics were in the Badlands, very near Medora, near the cabin of Teddy Roosevelt. There are a few families still out there, who remember meeting him. The roads today are beautiful; in the past, we had mud and alkali mixed. The buffalo were numerous then and even today the pathways are there. We ate many wild berries along the Missouri. Today with improved methods there are better grain crops; cars and trucks provide transportation now. And now there are many motels for the convenience of the traveler, not just any sordid hotel in each town along the highways.

The sunshine and moonlight are brighter because of the bareness. There is much wind, dust and dirt. I hated it in the beginning; the wind made a song for me. When it is windy, it seems more so than even Chicago, and without the protection of buildings.

Twenty miles east of us in Dickinson, the "rich" relatives lived; they were quite prosperous, but they were still envious of us. These were two uncles and their wives (sisters of my mother). We in our town mixed with everyone while they were one-sided by themselves. This didn't make much sense to me. They were the sentimental kind by face, but still of suspicious nature. They actually had a fear of contamination through mixing with people of other faiths. So then they were lonely.

The biggest success for us was my husband's smile. Today, his smile would be called a million dollar smile. Age has faded some of that away. People did and do like him for that.

By the way, four of our five children were born in North Dakota. When Charlotte was born, my parents were still in Minneapolis. I was homesick, so came home to meet the stork. The second daughter, Alice, was also born at my parents' home, but this time in Hebron, North Dakota. The folks then lived (before building their own home) upstairs of their store — a horrible, drafty, drab, and dark place with half a dozen rooms. Alice Roosevelt was then the debutante in the White House, and so we named our chubby new baby Alice too. The third daughter was born in our own home in Belfield. At first came disappointment — we thought this would be a son, but it really didn't matter at all. This one was called Marian. Five years later came our first son, in the Dickinson Hospital. This was my first trip to a hospital for that purpose. I shall never forget the good service and care there. I enjoyed the sister nurses; they were very kind. The surprise of a boy was a very great one to all of us, so the long distance telephone was very busy, going in all directions. We forgot expenses that time. My father could not believe that I actually had a boy. Just as he was dressed, with the house slippers and unbuttoned shirt, he caught the local train to see for himself this new grandson. My father was always partial to boys until his middle age. Then he changed his mind. He called on the daughters for good or for bad services. Then sixteen months later our baby boy, Gerald, arrived.

That year we had a very strong flu sickness all over the country. It was 1918. The only doctor in our town, a Dr. Spear, was engaged, but he developed a bad infection in his hand. So he called Doctor Scherbaum of Hebron to help him out. I was taken to Hebron, among all the confusion and noise of so many others, for this last baby. Dr. Scherbaum said to Dr. Spear, "What a smart owl you are." He accepted me just the same, with one condition — not to call him until I was sure the baby was arriving. Hebron was full of flu too. There were no nurses; the doctor took two of my sisters, Esther and Ruth, and made them emergency nurses. He prepared them in white and had hot water ready. The girls were frightened to death. When the baby arrived, the doctor explained each phase of birth, and also explained the birth of twins. Everything came out fine. My sister Anna of Bismarck had her first child, Milton three weeks earlier. Milton had the colic so the circumcision was delayed. She came with the baby to Hebron, and we had a double circumcision, with Rabbi Hyman of Minneapolis officiating, in the midst of all the family confusion.

In Belfield, the Presbyterian Church was getting a new minister. His name was Mutchnik. They were a young married couple. The headlines of our Belfield papers were saying "He comes to see, whether he Likes You, not Whether we Like HIM." They stayed close to five years. The pay was low. The Mutchniks were interested in the youth of the town and wished to begin some reforms. The dancing of "cheek to cheek" did not appeal to their modest pious souls. They used to come to us very often and complain. The peculiar thing about them to us was that this couple were both of Jewish ancestry. The minister's father had been a convert from Judaism. His wife was a Methodist. Mrs. Mutchnik herself was a graduate and practicing physician, but she did no medical work in Belfield. They were there four to five years, and then the minister had a heart attack. They left the town without funds. Their older child was then expected, another came later. The minister came to see us because he owed over $20 for groceries. My husband told him to forget the small debt. However, a few months later the money was sent to us, and we were very surprised. Many years passed — over thirty in fact — and we had lost trace of them. Through some investigation, we learned that Mrs. Mutchnik was still living in St. Louis. One of my younger sisters, Blanche, happened to be there not long ago and went to see her. She was still a practicing physician at the age of seventy for the city public health department. Her son had married a Jewish girl; her daughter was teaching. I learned a lot from both of them in many different ways.

I always thought a person could live on a budget. It seems that I always ask "how much"; we thought to work out a useful budget, but the more children, the less budgeting. I made one mistake — I should have been on a salary; how much more independent I would have been. But my husband never asked me how much I spent, and that was a help. He used to brag to others how fast he could catch a train; I agreed with him for the moment, but he also forgot to tell that the shirt, tie, cuff buttons, and the packed bag were all set out on the bed by me.

Among our good friends of Belfield, we had all the fathers of the Catholic churches, Rev. Mutchnik of the Presbyterian Church, and Minister Rugland of the Norwegian Church. (The Ruglands, with but $100 a month church income, managed to send nine daughters and sons through college.) One afternoon, Father Rosseler and Rev. Mutchnik both were over; I thought the best thing to serve would be wine. So I did, but with Rev. Mutchnik's rheumatism, he refused to drink, and Father Rosseler felt that the Rev. Mutchnik was discourteous. When Father Rosseler took the second glass, he spoke sharply to the Reverend, who in turn said, "I will drink at your wedding, Father Rosseler." And then Father Rosseler answered with : "See here, you are not a Jew, nor a Christian." They parted with a good handshake and in good humor.

I have told you about my brother Charles' marriage. Next came Ben's, who was married in Hebron. The girl was from Minneapolis. My folks made a lovely wedding for them. The bride's name was Betty Dechter. Betty's father was not living, but her mother and her six other children came out to the wedding. It was a large and beautiful one; half of the people in the town were invited. At that time brother Ben was my father's partner in the business; Esther (another sister) was the buyer in the store. We even had the wedding cook brought out from Minneapolis. I went down with the babies, to help supervise the wedding. It was a big affair for this small town.

The second big wedding in Hebron was for sister Anna and her husband, Charles Rosen of Bismarck. She used to work and buy for my father too. This wedding was even larger and more outstanding — quite elegant with the men dressed in formal tails. There was a huge dinner, cooked by the same woman from Minneapolis, and a beautiful dance later. The orchestra was brought down from Bismarck; everyone wore lavish clothes (my own dress was from Helena, Montana). Fine champagne was served. One of the guests, an Aunt Esther from Eureka, N.D., changed dresses three times that one evening to show off her New York gowns; the last change — an all over jet black dress. The newspapers were full of descriptions of the wedding; all the out of town guests staying in the hotel or private homes as guests of my parents; the welcome was so great that the guests stayed three days. I came from this large family and there was always something to think about or look forward to happening.

Esther was married in Minneapolis to Bill Rosenzweig at his parents' home. My folks and I were the only ones down for this wedding. She was a beautiful bride.

Samuel married Etta Blank of Minneapolis. This was a simple service at his parents' home — the rest of the family of sisters and brothers were all in school. Some went from Hebron to the University of Minnesota. About 1922, my folks moved back to Minneapolis. By this time, brother Sam was a graduate lawyer; he had studied at the University of North Dakota.

Later Saul graduated at Minnesota as a lawyer; Ruth attended the University music school; a sister Frances became a teacher; Blanche, a teacher too. Maurice also graduated in law, and Tobette, from the library school.

Saul and Jeannette Goodman were married a couple years after he finished school and had set up his law practice in Glen Ullin. Ruth married Ben Kieffer; Frances married Dr. Max Goldberg, and Blanche his brother, Dr. Iz Goldberg — all those weddings were within six months, January to June 1927; all large and beautiful, with much detail given to proper procedures.

Unhappily, Frances was married but eight years; she became very sick and was gone from us when she was but 32. This was the first big family tragedy. She left her husband Max, and two fine children — Marvin, now a doctor, and Mimi, a teacher. Maurice married Janet Reuler of St. Paul and Tobette, the youngest, married Dr. George Doroshow of St. Paul. Again, these were large weddings, and there are special memories with each of them.

When my folks had returned to Minneapolis in 1922, they bought a huge old-fashioned home with four bedrooms and three porches. The front porch seemed to be the center for all the family — for problems and for joys. My father was then retired and mostly at home.

One by one, with each daughter and then the two boys, our family grew up. The oldest was in high school. It was our wish to give our children the education that both my husband and I had missed, and also to give them some Jewish education. We were usually the only Jewish family in Belfield. For a few years, Herbert Mackoff, a lawyer, and his sister Ethel Pomerance and her husband Sol lived there. We are still very good friends and see Herbert and Ethel occasionally. Sol died a few years ago after living with asthma so long. All I did was to teach the children the Ten Commandments the best way I knew how, and lived in hopes that someday we would move and have the children confirmed, according to our beliefs.

We lived in Belfield for fourteen years, and the time came when we took inventory of ourselves and found out we owed it to the children, even if it meant sacrificing our income, to return to our home city. We returned in June 1924; the older children were confirmed, and the boys had bar mitzvahs, though I regret that change for they should have continued their studies at the Temple and been confirmed.

We also bought a lovely four bedroom home in the Lynnhurst district, with all new furnishings. But the memories of old home and store at Belfield were not so easily forgotten. To this day, we speak of the home place there. Many changes were necessary to replace people in the store. We also had many aggravations from this move. It was difficult to plant ourselves back — good and bad memories were in our minds for a long time.

Not every Jewish immigrant from
Eastern Europe settled on the Eastern seaboard of North America.
Some — on the whole, hardy — souls made their way into
the North American interior and became residents and even
homesteaders in areas as remote as North Dakota.
Bessie Schwartz was of this latter group. Americans, she observed,
"love a hard country, but the West must be loved
as you love your family." She wrote these words in the mid-1950's, a
half-century after her arrival in the United States.

Origins

Moses Lasky

rving Howe, in his book *World of Our Fathers*,[1] tells how the great migration to the United States of East European Jewry began in 1881, following the assassination of Czar Alexander II early that year and the consequent pogroms. Marcus Arkin, in *Aspects of Jewish Economic History*,[2] tells us that somewhat independently a migration of Jewry from the much more tolerant Austro-Hungarian Empire began about the same time and that about 300,000 Jews came to the United States from Galicia alone, although there were no pogroms there. My father came to this country in 1883 from Galicia, then under Austrian control, and my mother came from Russian Poland in 1890.

Israel Joshua Singer, the elder brother of the more famous Yiddish author Isaac Bashevis Singer, tells us in his novel *Yoshe Kalb* of a race of redheaded Jews occupying the slopes of the Carpathian Mountains. My father was redheaded, and this is the area from which he came. (My brother Philip was redheaded, before graying, and my son and daughter are redheaded). My father came from or in the vicinity of the village of Mielec,[3] near Tarnow. He was born on December 2, 1867, and was thus 16 years old, when, by himself, he came to New York City.

An older brother of my father, Samuel (Sam), and a younger, Isaac (Ike), also came to this country, whether earlier or later I do not know for sure, though I believe that both came later.[4]

My father's name was Judah Eisen (in Hebrew, Judah ben Meir. It is from Meir that my sister Mary, the youngest of my father's nine children, derived the name Miriam and that my son Marshall obtained the same Hebrew name, Meyer).

Irving Howe retells the old story of the confusion of the immigrant coming through Castle Garden, New York City. (Ellis Island did not become the immigrant's point of entry until years later). The immigrant had to give evidence that he would not become a public burden. As I recall my mother telling, my 16-year-old father gave as a reference the name of one aunt named Laskowitz, who lived somewhere in this country,[5] and the immigration officials thereupon entered his name as Juda Laskowitz. Thus he lost his own name for many years. Somewhere along the line, the name "Juda" was Americanized to Joe, and until 1924 my father was known as Joe Laskowitz.

As a boy in New York City, he earned his living making cane bottoms for chairs and peddling them in the streets. Sometime before 1887, he came to Denver, Colorado, probably because he then had a sister there. (How and when she came there I have never heard.) My father took out his first naturalization papers in Denver on July 6, 1887, before he was 21; he became a citizen in 1894. Standing on cane-bottomed chairs, he was in the retail furniture business, possibly secondhand, but left this business before I was old enough to remember. In the possession of one of my brothers is a medal of the Knights of the Maccabees, a Jewish counterpart of the Knights of Columbus, "presented by the Supreme Tent to J. Laskowitz as a hustling Maccabee 7-15-03."

My father and mother were married at Denver on July 19, 1897, when he was 29. He had been married before, when he was 23, to a woman whose name I never knew. It was a situation common enough among traditionalist Jews, but would have been extraordinary for the 1890's in an American setting, for it was he who obtained the divorce from her, which was most unusual for an age when divorces were uncommon among Americans and American husbands did not sue the wife. By his first marriage he had three children, the eldest a daughter named Nettie, and two sons, Jacob or Jake (later called Jack), and another named Louis (Lew), who later chose to use the English spelling Lewis. A newly married girl in her mid-twenties, my mother assumed the care of Jack and Lew, ages 5 and 2, and reared them. Nettie went with her mother, and I do not recall ever even meeting her until I was in my forties.

The world of Irving Howe's fathers is not my world. The background of American Jews as Howe describes it is not mine. With its East European origins, it is, but it diverged rapidly. My mother never experienced the New York scene, and my father soon left it.

My mother's maiden name was Grossman. She was born on October 16, 1871, and came to the United States, directly to Denver, in the 1890's, accompanied by a younger sister, Yetta, to visit a brother, Max. Somewhere in this country, her good Hebrew name, Chia (meaning "life"), became the Greek name Ida.

My father's parents were peddlers to the peasants around Mielec. My mother came from a line of rabbis on her father's side and of merchant princes on her mother's side, or so the tradition goes as I heard it as a small boy. Irving Howe tells us how, among East European Jewry, the brilliant young student of the Talmud was the catch for the daughters of the wealthy. My maternal grandmother, Rachel,[6] was the daughter of a family named Friedman, engaged in distilling alcohol and selling wheat, a business taken over by my maternal grandfather. I recall my mother's telling me of reverses in the family fortune when a shipload of grain sank in the Vistula River. The Friedmans and the Grossmans lived in the town of Ostrowa in the government district of Lomza—Lomza Gobiernya—about fifty-five kilometers northeast of Warsaw, then under Russian control. In September, 1977, I engaged a car and driver to take me to Ostrowa from Warsaw. The round trip took some six or seven hours, including an hour and a half in Ostrowa. The country is flat and thinly forested; Ostrowa is a small country town. It was part of the Generalgouvernement (Nazi-occupied Poland); and a center of partisan resistance to Hitler in World War II. Its oldest building was the town hall, built in 1927. I was unable to associate that drab town with the tradition of a wealthy industrialist.[7]

Among my possessions are a photograph of my mother's parents, Meir and Sarah, and a photograph of her mother's parents, Israel and Rachel. Meir and Sarah are obviously of peasant stock, and from them must have come the qualities of endurance and self-reliance which I associate with my father. Israel and Rachel are obviously cultured aristocrats so far as a Jew in Eastern Europe could be an aristocrat, and from Israel must have come the intelligence I associate with my mother. In the eighteenth century and early nineteenth century, Hasidism swept the poor Jews of Eastern Europe in an ecstatic emotional version of Judaism.[8] They were opposed by the Misnagdim, who adhered to the traditional, scholarly Talmud-oriented Judaism. The Grossmans and the Friedmans were Misnagdim.

In Eastern Europe, I have heard or read, the duty of Jewish boys and girls was to marry and beget children, particularly among the wealthy. The duty probably arose from the teaching of medieval Jewish mysticism—the kabbalistic Zohar or the teachings of Isaac Luria of Safed—that in the beginning God created once and for all the full quota of souls, and the day of judgment will arrive when the last of them has been given a body. To hasten that blessed day, the young must marry and beget.

Zohar, Luria, or whatever, my mother was the seventeenth of twenty-two children.[9] Israel Grossman, the rabbi's son, was born about 1827, and was age 13 when he was married to Rachel Friedman, then age 16. They lived together for eighty years, both dying in the same year, when he was 93 and she was 96. They died of hunger in the midst or aftermath of World War I, when Poland was successively overrun and ravaged by Germans, Czarist Russians, Polish revolutionaries, Bolsheviks, and Petlurist Ukrainians, all of whom detested the Jews even more.

Grandmother Rachel peers forth from her photograph, prim and severe. She must have spent her life as a brood mare. My mother recounted little of her and remembered being raised by nurses. Grandfather Israel peers out pleasant and kindly; my mother recalled him with affection. (Meir and Sarah look out of their photograph, poor and tired).

Her brother Max, as my mother related it, was the "black sheep" of the family; those are her words.[10] For some reason, he emigrated to America, wrote back home of gold in the streets, and invited his two favorite sisters, Chia and Yetta, to visit him. They found that he was a poor cigar maker, and they never returned home. Within a short time she met my father and married him; from old pictures, he looked like my son, Marshall.

My mother had six children and reared eight. I was my mother's fifth and last son and my father's seventh, born November 2, 1907. One more child, my late sister Mary, was born September 14, 1909. The other sons were Abraham William (Will), born in April 1898 (still alive); George, born in 1899 (died in November 1978); Samuel, born in July 1901 (died in February 1964), named after my father's brother Samuel; and Philip, born February 12, 1906 (still alive). I was named Moses after an uncle (my mother's brother), who died a few weeks before I was born.

My father had a sister, Hannah or Anne.[11] When she arrived in this country, I do not know. She was married to a man named Adolph Alpert, and Alpert's destiny became entwined with the course of empire and affected mine. In the early part of the century, David (?) Moffat promoted the building of a railroad from Denver, over the Continental Divide through Northwest Colorado, destined to Salt Lake City. Officially named the Denver and Salt Lake Railroad, it was popularly called the "Moffat Line" or "Moffat Road." It never got beyond Craig, Colorado, and in the 1930's by a bypass southerly to the Denver and Rio Grande Western, reached Salt Lake City over the D&RG Western tracks, there joining up with the Western Pacific to the West Coast. Before 1910 the Moffat Road had reached and stopped at a village called Kremmling, Colorado, 126 rail miles from Denver, located on the western slope of the Rockies, lying between Granby (by Grand Lake on the other side of the Divide from Estes Park) and Steamboat Springs. Kremmling lies in Grand County, in "Middle Park,"[12] on the bank of what was then called Grand River, one of the tributaries of the Colorado River, now called the Colorado River itself.

As the terminus of the railroad, the point from which the line was being extended, and as a supply point for cattle ranchers, Kremmling drew Adolph Alpert to open Alpert's Department Store, a general merchandise store that sold everything from pins up and supplied the ranchers on credit each year until the cattle were sold. When, in 1976, Kremmling celebrated its centennial in conjunction with the American Bicentennial, it invited Adolph Alpert's son, Joe (whom I have never met), as an honored guest.

About 1909, Adolph Alpert died of tuberculosis, and his widow Hannah asked her brother, my father, to take over the store.[13] This he did, in 1910, purchasing it in 1912, and changing its name to North Western Mercantile Company. A letterhead dated 8/30/13 describes the North Western Mercantile Co. as handling "Gents' and Ladies' Furnishings, Staple and Fancy Groceries, Shelf and Heavy Hardware and Farm Implements, Full Line of Furniture."

Thus it was that, in 1913, at the age of 6, having gone through kindergarten in Denver, I found myself in the first grade in Kremmling.

Kremmling had board sidewalks, elevated high off the dirt street level to make it easy for the cowboys to mount their horses. Each home drew its water from a well by pulley and bucket or, if affluent, like the mayor's, by pump. Lighting was by kerosene lamp or, for Northwestern Mercantile Company, by gasoline vapor and Welsbach mantle similar to the Coleman lamp. The needs of nature were served by the outhouse.[14] Bathing was in a circular, galvanized washtub about two feet in diameter, mounted on two kitchen chairs, with the water heated in a galvanized oval boiler on a wood or soft coal-fired kitchen stove (Coal was mined not far away).

The elementary school consisted of an old barn converted into two rooms (Later, my father became secretary of the school board and urged it into building a "real" brick school, but that was after I had passed out of the elementary school). In one room of the converted barn, grades one through four were taught by one teacher; in the other room, grades five through eight, by the principal. I was able to learn all that room one had to offer in one or two years and all that room two had to offer in another year or two. Soon after, for some reason which I do not recall,[15] my mother spent a year in Denver, so that I had to squander a whole year in the fifth grade in Denver in the old Gilpin school.

At age 10 I was ready for high school. The Kremmling high school served a large surrounding area. It was held on the top or second floor of the Town Hall, a small brick structure in the middle of the town square. The ground floor of the Town Hall was occupied by the equipment of the volunteer fire department; the town pump was in front of the building, and across the street were the town's two saloons. Joe Allen's and Emil Schlumpf's (probably the town brothels also, a fact that did not dawn on me until years later).

My mother was determined that I should have a better education than the Kremmling high school offered, and she moved to Denver. There, at the age of 10, in the fall of 1918, I entered the ninth grade and was graduated from East Denver High School in 1922.

Living alone in Kremmling was too much for my father, and about 1920 he sold the Northwestern Mercantile Company and moved to Denver. I have since thought that the desire to give me an education was an economic misfortune for him. After giving up his business in Kremmling, he engaged in a number of relatively unsuccessful enterprises, an automobile tire store and then a men's clothing store. The land and building of the Northwestern Mercantile Company he sold, as I have since learned, for $2,000. In 1976 the present owner rejected $100,000 for the land. In 1930, after I had settled in San Francisco, my parents moved there, and he returned to his old business of furniture. My mother died in 1933, and my father in 1936.

About 1920, my half-brother Lew, a traveling salesman, shortened the name Laskowitz to Lasky, and my brother George soon did so also. When I matriculated at the University of Colorado (Boulder) in the fall of 1922 at age 14 (on scholarship), I chose the name Lasky and was accepted under that name. My father felt no loyalty to the name Laskowitz, which had been foisted on him in 1883, and in 1924 he obtained a court order changing his name back to Judah Eisen but adding Lasky, thus taking the name chosen by all his sons.

———

Moses Lasky, San Francisco attorney, has been president of the San Franciso Museum of Art and a member of the national executive committee of the American Jewish Committee. This memoir recalls his childhood in an East European immigrant family which settled in Colorado nearly a century ago.

———

Notes

1. New York: Harcourt, Brace, Jovanovich, 1976.
2. Philadelphia: Jewish Publication Society of America, 1976.
3. I deduce my father's birthplace as Mielec from the fact that my mother told me, when I was a small boy, that he came from a village near Tarnow, and among papers I have from my parent's effects is a photograph of my father's parents with the photographer's name and his address as Mielec. There is that town in Poland still, not too far from Cracow.
4. I have met neither. Sam died before my father, and Ike was living in Florida until a few years ago. I have met Ike's son, Ben, a New York City lawyer, and Ike's daughter, Sue.
5. I have never heard anything more about this aunt.
6. Recently my brother Philip, constructing a genealogic tree, has come up with the idea that our maternal grandmother's name was something else. My memory that our mother told me that the name was Rachel is vivid, clear, and unshakeable.
7. I also reserved a car and driver to take me from Cracow to Mielec on a Sunday, but the driver never showed up, and the trip was never made. He probably got drunk on Saturday night. The terrain from Cracow toward Mielec is rolling foothills on the northern slopes of the Carpathians.
8. As a boy, on reading Graetz and other histories of the Jews, I thought of the Hasidim as Jewish "Holy Rollers." Martin Buber has made them respectable.
9. This is my memory of what my mother said. Recently a cousin has said that my mother

was the youngest. That cannot be, for her sister Yetta was younger, although my mother may not have been the seventeenth. I may have confused her rank with the statement that seventeen of the twenty-two grew up to have families of their own. There must have been hundreds of cousins destroyed by Hitler, leaving only some in the United States and England.

10. Why a "black sheep," I never knew. I was very fond of the two of his children whom I knew well.

11. Of another sister, Rose, I have encountered but one reference.

12. The French fur trappers years before called the high open areas between the ranges "parks." In Colorado there are North Park, Middle Park, and South Park. Aspen is in South Park.

13. I have a deed of indenture between my father and his sister, in 1912, indenturing my brother Lew to her to serve for room, board and training.

14. I used to wonder how my mother stood this, but having seen Ostrowa, now conclude that life as a girl in the 1870's could only have been different by degrees.

15. My brothers George and Sam were attending high school in Denver, boarding, and it may be that my mother felt that she should be with them.

Index

Uri D. Herscher is Professor of American Jewish History
at the Los Angeles campus of the Hebrew Union College–Jewish Institute
of Religion. He is the author of A Socialist Perspective
on Jews, America and Immigration *(with Stanley F. Chyet) and* Jewish
Agricultural Utopias in America, 1880-1910.

Monographs of the American Jewish Archives

1

Jewish Americana (1954)

2

An American Jewish Bibliography by Allan E. Levine (1959)

3

Reference to Jews in the Newport Mercury, 1758-1786
by Irwin S. Rhodes (1961)

4

The Theology of Isaac Mayer Wise by Andrew F. Key (1962)

5

Manual of the American Jewish Archives by David M. Zielonka (1966)

6

*Selected Items of American Jewish Interest in the Yiddish Periodicals
of Russia and Poland, 1862-1940* by Leo Shpall (1966)

7

*Commerce and Contraband in New Orleans during the French
and Indian War* by A.P. Nasatir and James R. Mills (1968)

8

The Jews of Coro, Venezuela by Isaac S. Emmanuel (1973)

9

*A Century of Memories: The East European Jewish Experience
in America,* Edited by Uri D. Herscher (1982)

10

*Among the Survivors of the Holocaust–1945
The Landsberg DP Camp Letters of Major Irving Heymont,
United States Army* (1982)